Management
Say it with fun

My way of joking is to tell the truth.

George Bernard Shaw

Cartoonist Gopulu has to his credit a host of engaging hilarious pieces in the popular Tamil weekly *Ananda Vikatan* for two decades since 1945. Most of them are non-verbal. Like music, they transcend language barriers. He has been honoured deservingly by Tamil Nadu Government and various literary and social bodies. This book carries as many as 278 cartoons, subtly intrepreted by Dr. R. Natarajan.

Dr. R. Natarajan, who has articulated Gopulu's pantomimes with his cryptic one-liners from management angle, is a Professor, Consultant and award-winning bi-lingual author. He has served the media, academia, US diplomatic mission and corporate sector for over four decades.

Management
Say it with fun

Gopulu
&
R. Natarajan

MJP Publishers

Cataloguing-in-Publication Data

Gopalan, S (1924-   ).
Management: Say it with fun / by S. Gopalan [and]
R. Natarajan. - Chennai : MJP Publishers, 2012
xxii, 278p.; 21 cm.
ISBN 978-81-8094-128-3 (pb.)
1. Management, Jokes 2. Jokes-Managers 3. English Jokes, Managers
I. Natarajan, R II. Title.
820.802 08623 dc 22 GOP MJP 104

ISBN 978-81-8094-128-3   **MJP PUBLISHERS**
© Publishers, 2012   New No. 5, Muthu Kalathy Street
All rights reserved   Triplicane
Printed and bound in India   Chennai 600 005

Publisher : J.C. Pillai
Managing Editor : C. Sajeesh Kumar
Project Editor : P. Parvath Radha
Acquisitions Editor : C. Janarthanan
Editorial Team : B. Ramalakshmi, V.R. Padma, Lissy John,
R. Hemalatha, M. Gnanasoundari,
B. Annalakshmi, S. Jeevasruthi
CIP Data : Prof. K. Hariharan, Librarian
RKM Vivekananda College, Chennai.

A remarkable job

Let me confess, I tried to create my own captions for the brilliant cartoons of Shri Gopulu. I thought, if my friend Mr. Natarajan can do, I can do it as well. But I failed. I was not able to think of even one caption, and I gave it up after some serious attempts.

Mr. Natarajan is known to me for several years and I had the privilege of publishing many of his articles in our journal *Thuglak*. He has a very subtle sense of humour with which he demolishes the present-day politicians without their even realizing that they have been bruised badly.

And that subtle sense of humour is seen in every caption that Mr. Natarajan had given to Gopulu's jokes. That these cartoons can be interpreted managerially is in itself a brilliant thought.

Mr. Natarajan has done a remarkable job and I do not want to commit a fault about which he has warned in one of his captions: *"Don't overdo the preliminaries."* I shall not.

Cho. S. Ramaswamy
Editor, *Thuglak*

Publisher's Note

Cartoons are popular and powerful media expressions, depicting the contemporary political and socio-economic scenario. They present current affairs humorously. Being topical, they are generally considered period products.

Contrarily, Gopulu, a celebrity Tamil caricaturist, created all-time classics for about 20 years in the popular Tamil weekly *Ananda Vikatan*. Being pantomimes, silent jokes, they could be enjoyed in magazines of any language. With Dr. R. Natarajan's crisp, humorous one-liners, they are transformed here as illustrated management lessons.

There do exist illustrated books in the management den. But this is genetically different. While cartoons of other books depict management thoughts of an author, here a cartoonist's silent impressions of the behaviour of people are articulated by an author from the management angle.

This revival of a celebrity's jokes of the past, infused with modern managerial bearings, will serve as a pictorial guide to practising managers and also as an effective, illustrated textbook to the students in business schools.

We thank *Ananda Vikatan* for granting permission to use Sri Gopulu's cartoons for this value-added edition.

MJP Publishers

Foreword

Cartoonist Gopulu was a household name in the '50s and the '60s and specially for the readers of *Ananda Vikatan*. He was an avidly looked-forward-to weekly delight. Only a genius like him can convey in a few lines and sketches a world of meaning.

Four decades later, Dr. R. Natarajan, a multifarious personality, with a passion for the written word has verbalized Gopulu's drawings from the management angle with a sensitivity and an understatement that enhances the appeal of the original but at the same time compels one to appreciate and absorb the interpretation.

At the best of times, interpretation is a difficult task, more so when the original is an unspoken word. Dr. R. Natarajan has succeeded brilliantly in this difficult task.

N. Gopalaswami, IAS (Retd.)
Former Chief Election Commissioner

A creative duo

Veteran cartoonist Shri Gopulu's jokes entertained my generation. When *Vikatan* published some of his cartoons recently, none expected R. Natarajan would add a witty text. Natarajan spends his time with me everyday. I know that in a couple of days of his buying Gopulu's book, he wrote all his one-liners. Gopulu gave the seed. Natarajan nursed it. I admire both.

Nalli Kuppuswami Chettiar
Silk Industrialist

Laugh and muse

Gopulu is a genial cartoonist and R. Natarajan, in contrast, is a biting political satirist. But the two happily co-exist here. This is not one book, but two, seemlessly fused into one—the jokes of Gopulu and the one-liners of R. Natarajan.

It is a product of two mighty minds. But the creative geniuses did not work together for this. Gopulu drew these silent jokes par excellence in *Ananda Vikatan* five decades ago and Natarajan, of his son's age, has articulated them now as management tips.

Making pantomimes of the past speak eloquently and relevantly is a formidable challenge. Natarajan has met it with an inimitable ease. None can wield a wittier pen. Gopulu has carved his niche in the media; Natarajan has etched him in the management den.

In interpreting men and matters, by lines and between the lines, the two worthies revel in hilarious harmony. Here truth is recommended by humour and humour is sustained by truth. That is the cardinal characteristic of the best piece of literature. This book is one.

Bhakkiam Ramasami
(J.R. Sundaresan)
Humorist

This silence is heard

To those who wish to learn management through jokes, I commend this book. Gopulu's silence is sweet, Natarajan's eloquence is sweeter, as he is a litterateur and a management consultant.

As a Professor of Management, I wish to carry to classrooms the cartoons of Gopulu on Power Point and elicit students' comments. Then I will treat them to Natarajan's managerial interpretations. It will help students grasp management nuances better.

Management institutions can cover the content in MBA curriculum. The book is an excellent course material for HR workshops/seminars.

Satheesh Krishnamurthy
Professor, IIPM, Chennai

My fun and his pen

My non-verbal jokes in the popular Tamil weekly, *Ananda Vikatan,* week after week for nearly two decades were sugar candies, as readers termed them. They have now turned lollipops, with a management handle from my friend Dr. R. Natarajan. Thanks to his witty pen, my pantomimes are now eloquent.

With admirable insight Natarajan has grasped the subtleties of my cartoons. I am delighted to see them so re-incarnated. His creativity has turned my vintage vignettes into management lessons. In verbalizing the non-verbal, in elucidating the vestiges of the past, I am happy that Natarajan has made the first ever attempt of creative revivalism in our media annals. I commend him for that.

I thank *Ananda Vikatan,* which published about 280 of my cartoons as a cute booklet. It prompted Dr. Natarajan to provide a value addition with consummate ease.

I am equally thankful to Shri N. Gopalaswami, IAS (Retd.), our former Chief Election Commissioner, for his Foreword to this book. His commendation is noteworthy, as he is a management expert himself. He managed India, as our excellent Home Secretary. He shouldered heavy responsibilities with sagacity and humour. I thank Sri Cho Ramaswamy and Bhakkiam Ramasami for commending this work. It is evident that these eminent persons have enjoyed the Gopulu–Natarajan combine.

The book is aptly titled *Management: Say it with Fun.* While the fun is mine, the say is Natarajan's. This is a novelty. I commend him for his creativity in carrying me to the next generation's readers.

Gopulu

Preface

Elderly readers of the popular Tamil weekly *Ananda Vikatan* remember stalwarts who conceived jokes and illustrated them, like the celluloid heroes and heroines of yesteryears who sang and delivered dialogue. Nowadays one conceives the joke and another illustrates it. Sri Gopulu, a creative genius nearing 90, has served *Vikatan* as a staff cartoonist for about two decades. He sketched every week pantomimes—jokes sans words—which portray life's ironies and oddities as he observed.

Recently Vikatan brought out a selection of Gopulu's jokes. Those of my age group have enjoyed them in the1950s and 1960s. On second reading, I found the connotations interesting. No man forgets his original trade. Having taught English and Management, I have flashed here the management lessons I could cull out from them.

Engrossed by Sri Gopulu's succinct observation of life's funs and foibles, I wrote my one-liners overnight. I revised a few later. Where two words sufficed, I did not tag the third, since brevity is the soul of wit. I circulated my dummy among friends in different fields. I received encouraging comments from them.

Some of these are period jokes. A turbaned person (213) dipping his pen in the coffee cup and not in the ink pot is one. Fountain pens came later. Clotheslines in orthodox houses (250) were poles in those days and the handler used another pole for placing and taking clothes. Joke 58 relates to policemen. Cyclists were not allowed to carry one on the pillion in those days. Cyclists should not go without lamp (166) in night. These were punishable offences. A few more jokes like man-hauled rickshaws (140) may look strange to the younger generation. My comments accord them contemporaneity.

The whole world may be pleased, but if Gopulu is not, my work is not worth a wee bit. Therefore I was eager to show the dummy to Sri Gopulu. I had a brief interaction with him in 1984 for a booklet on health for Neyveli Lignite Corporation. The text was mine; sketches were his. I thought he would have forgotten it. So I requested writer Ranimaindan to set up an appointment with him.

Sri Gopulu, of my father's age, put me at ease and recalled the work for NLC. He flipped through the dummy. I was prepared even for admonition. If he said, "Hi, my jokes are pantomimes. Silence is their strength. Don't mar them verbally," I would have buried my labour of love then and there. But a mystified Gopulu said, "I never expected this. Anyhow, give me a couple of days."

Sri Gopulu called me later and said my attempt was 'unique' and he enjoyed my one-liners, though he did not intend them so. His nod was 'Brahma Rishi' title from Vasishta.

I thank doyen cartoonist Gopulu, for the liberties he granted in articulating his pantomimes, Sri N. Gopalaswami, IAS (Retd), former Chief Election Commissioner, who has graced a Foreword, my friend and patron Padma Shri Nalli Kuppuswami Chettiar, noted humorists Sri Cho. Ramaswamy and Sri Bhakkiam Ramasami, and

Prof. Satheesh Krishnamurthy, IIPM, for their commendations.

I thank *Ananda Vikatan,* for permission to this annotated edition. The speed with which the work started, it should have come out earlier. My prior engagements caused the delay. MJP Publishers, Chennai, specializing in management titles, took interest in this. Artist Aras, an admirer of Gopulu, did the cover cartoon. I thank Aras and MJP Publishers for their interest in this.

R. Natarajan

Every solution brings in
a fresh problem.

You don't pass for
as you pose for.

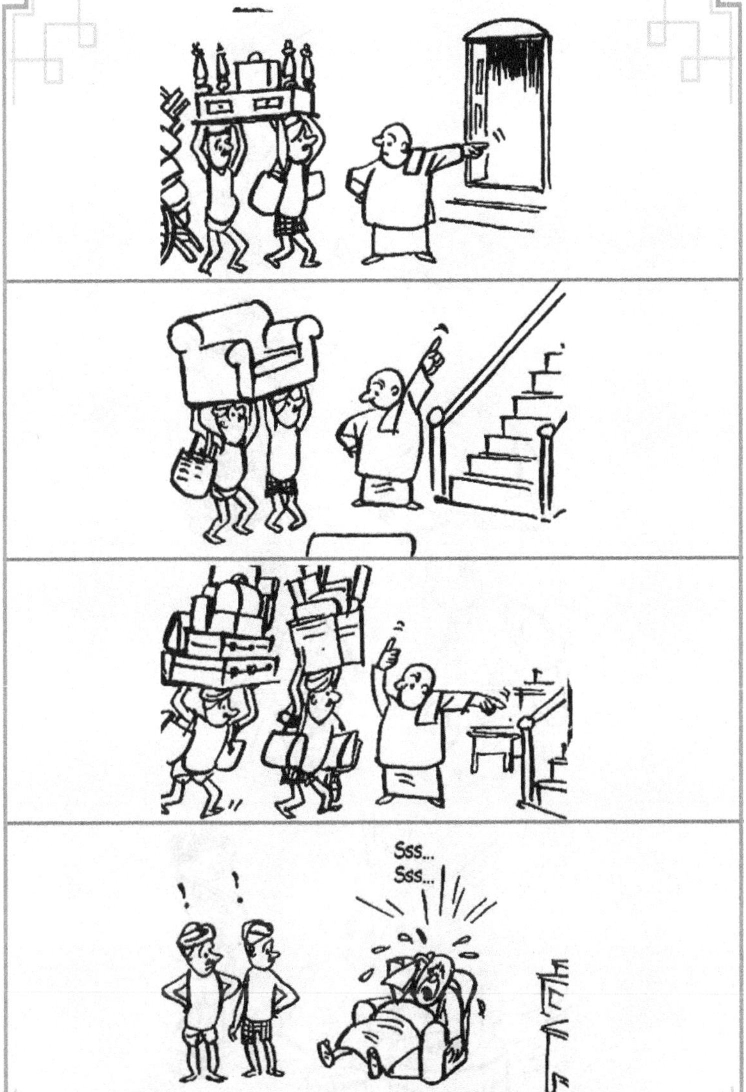

Work tires; supervising tires more.

No artiste is a hero to his partner.

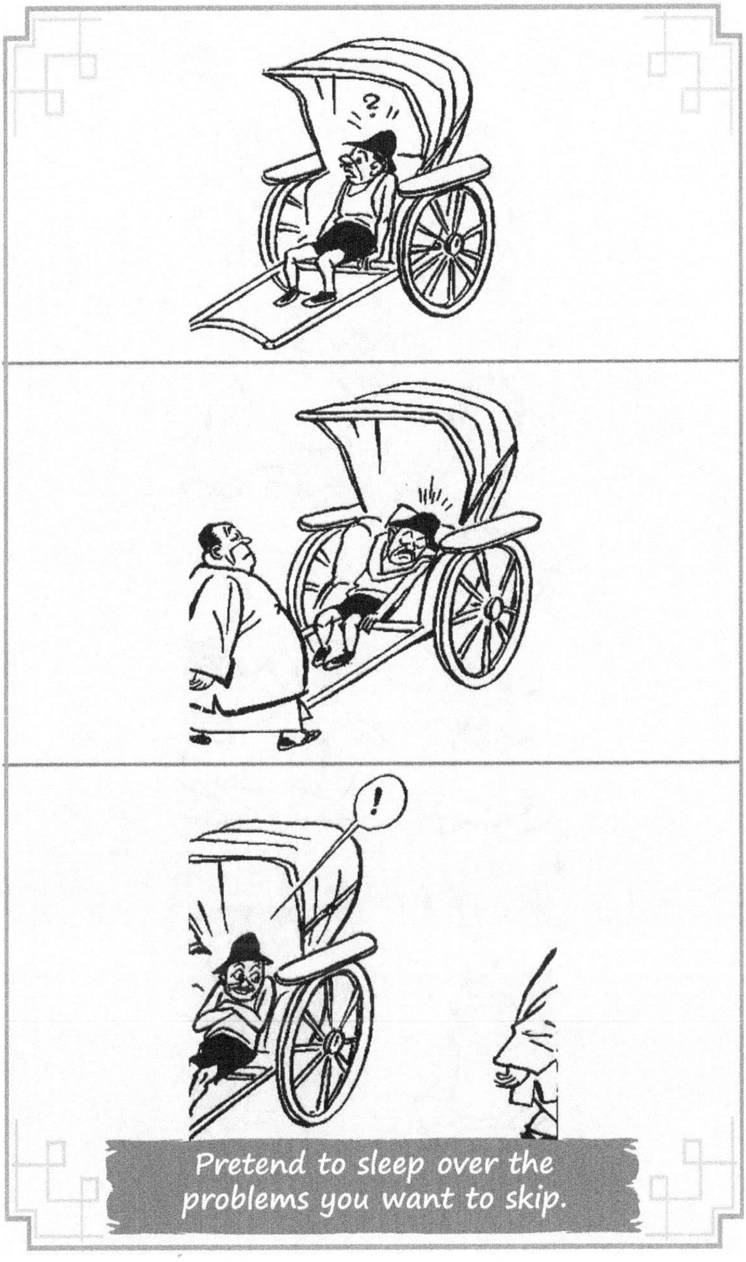

Pretend to sleep over the
problems you want to skip.

In tears lie the cheers.

You cannot always win
by an aided focus.

Where you rush
to save, you lose.

When the oral fails,
flash the verbal.

The other side of the wall is
no different from yours.

Your pastime lies far from
your professional den.

Few tap timely help at hand.

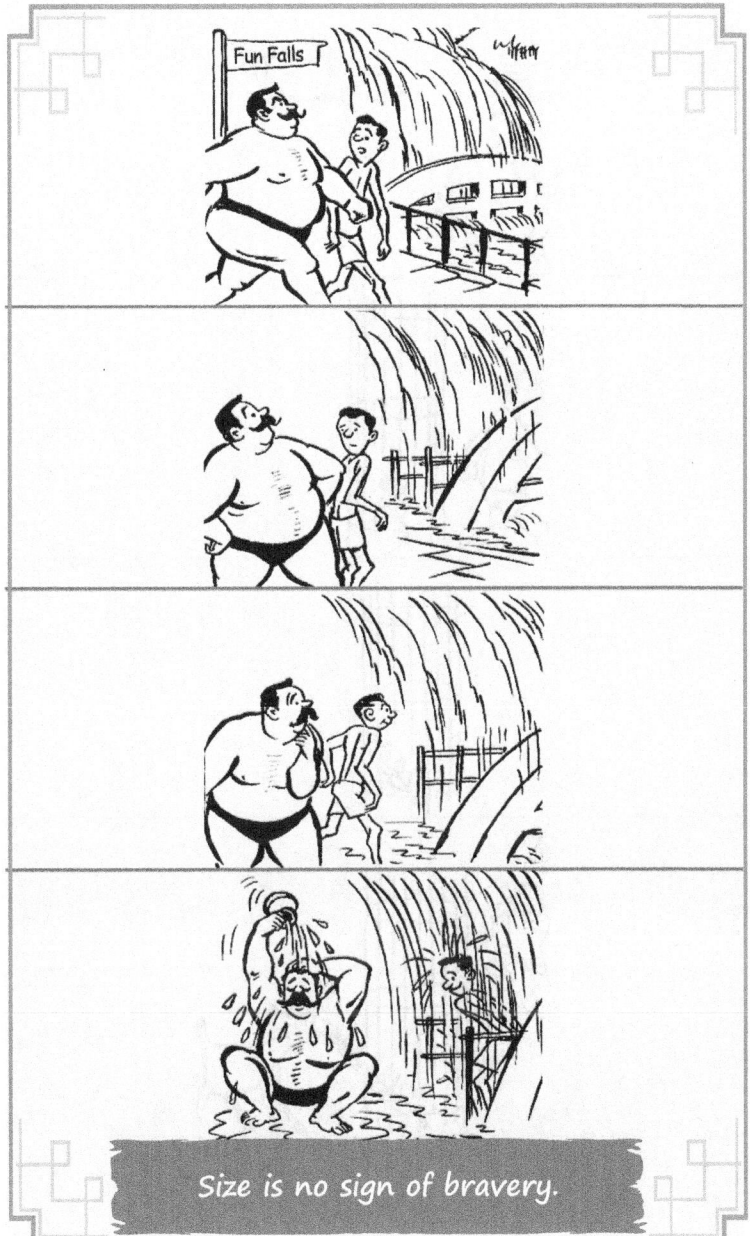

Size is no sign of bravery.

Fence is no defence.

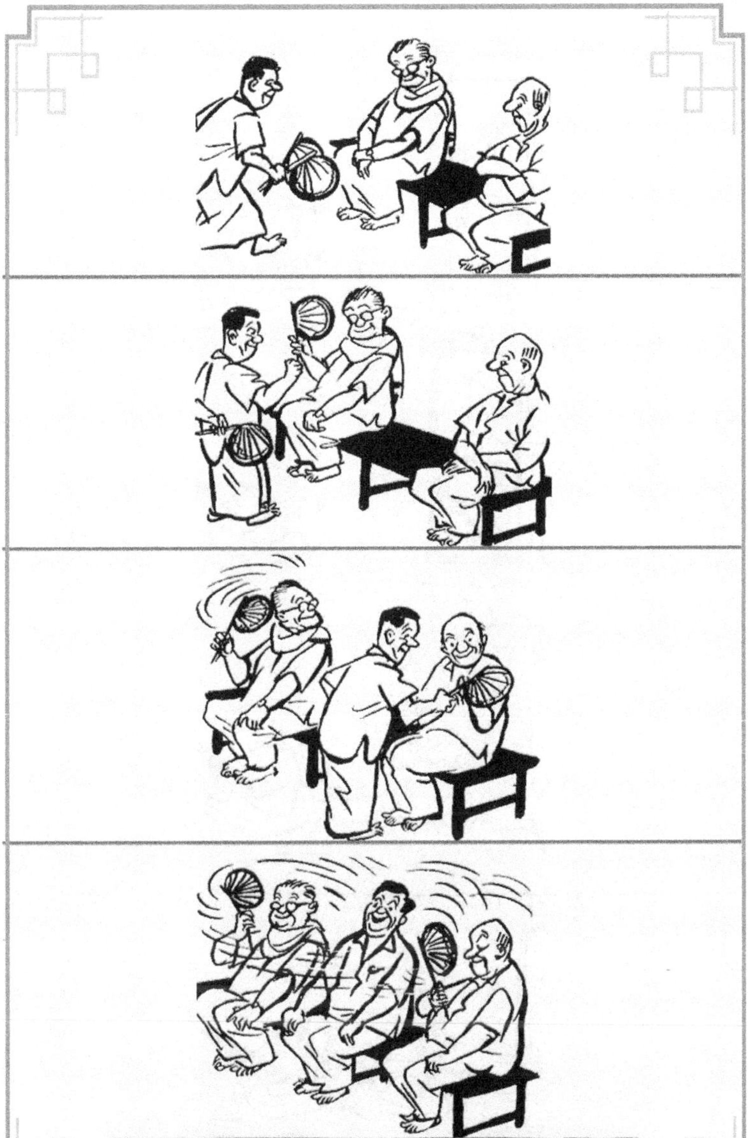

Help others and
be doubly helped.

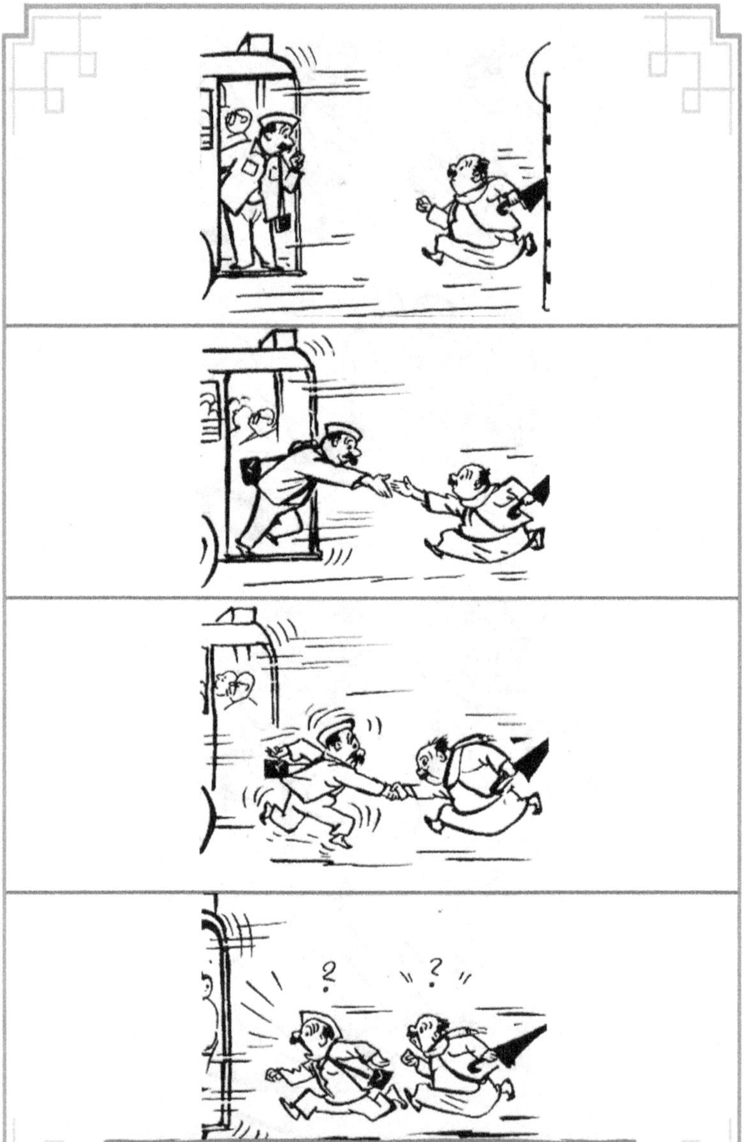

Your helping hand
might unseat you.

Elusive when sought; embarrassing later—Kids and targets.

Sleep knows no discomfort,
nor does comfort coax one to sleep.

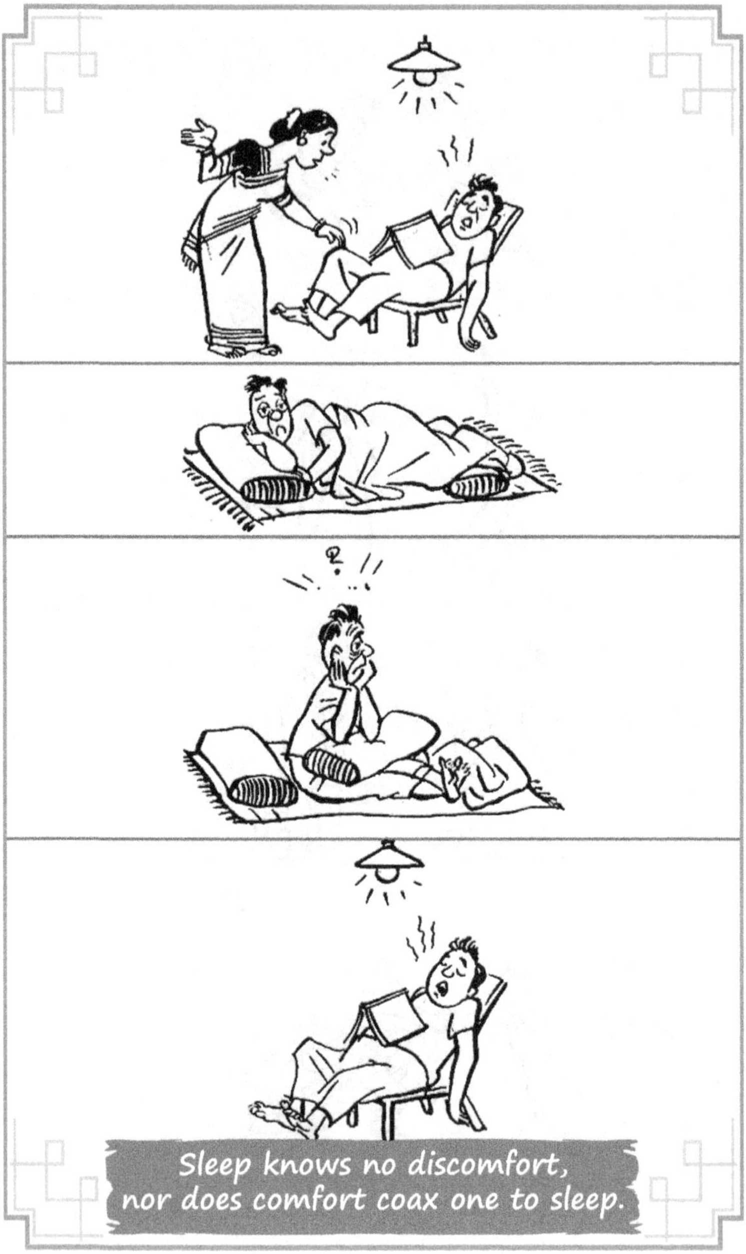

With alms the premium, charity is insurance cover.

Some hindrances blow up
when you try to remove them.

An astrologer consults
his own astrologer.

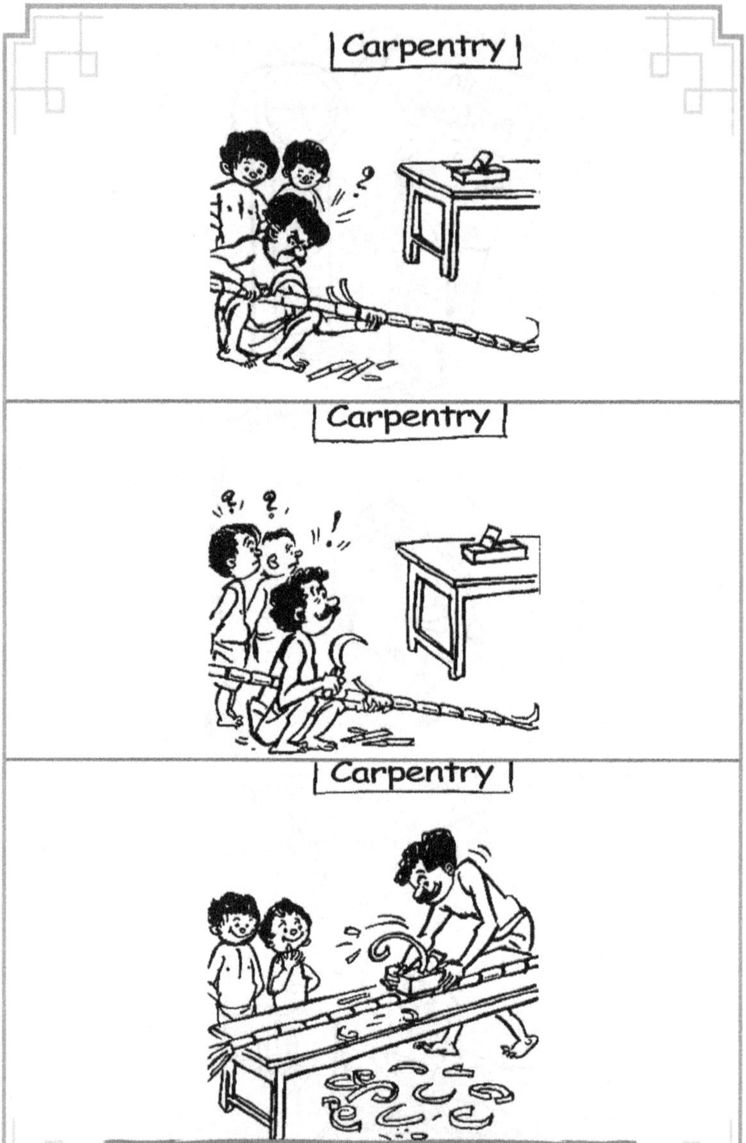

| Carpentry |

| Carpentry |

| Carpentry |

Old tools find new uses.

Don't wax your moustache when your wife waxes her eloquence.

The target: not you,
but your possessions.

The thief is cleverer
than the cop.

Modernise tradition
with a value addition.

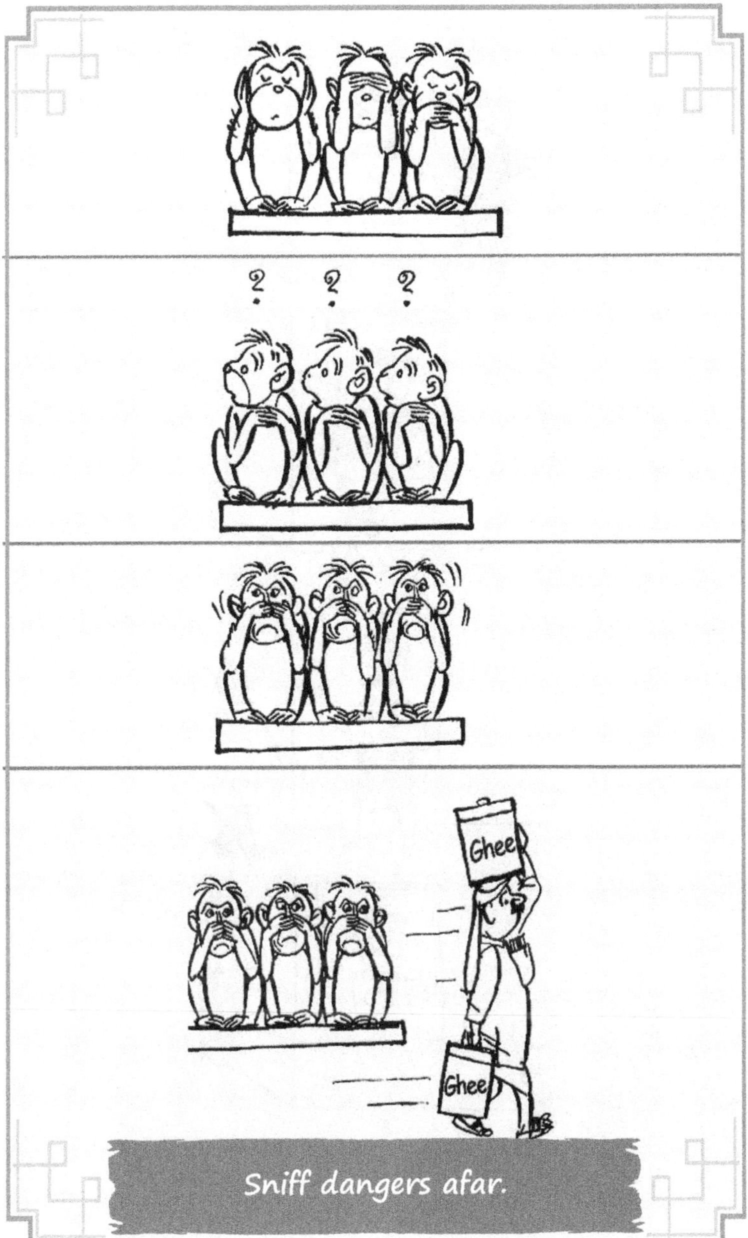

Sniff dangers afar.

Clone yourself to fool the one on prowl.

Learn by example.

Rigour might follow relief.

If you suspect something to collapse, it will.

Fancying is fine till
you face the reality.

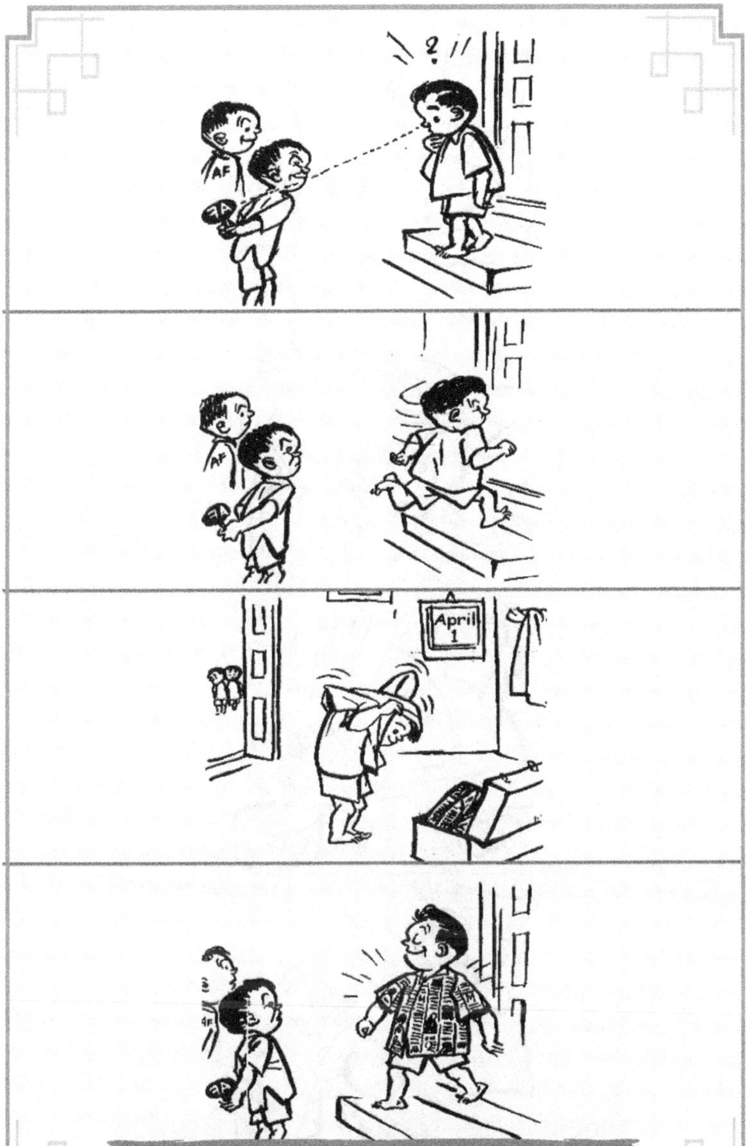

The smart pre-empt pranks.

Win the enemy
in his own way.

Even lesser mortals
are cleverer.

A make-believe
backdrop counts.

In sharing the spoils who bothers
the mishap or the victim?

Cut the supply chain,
to be heard.

Harsh handling of peripherals damages the core.

Cavalry ranks and robes
do not count at home.

Unsolicited mediation is risky.

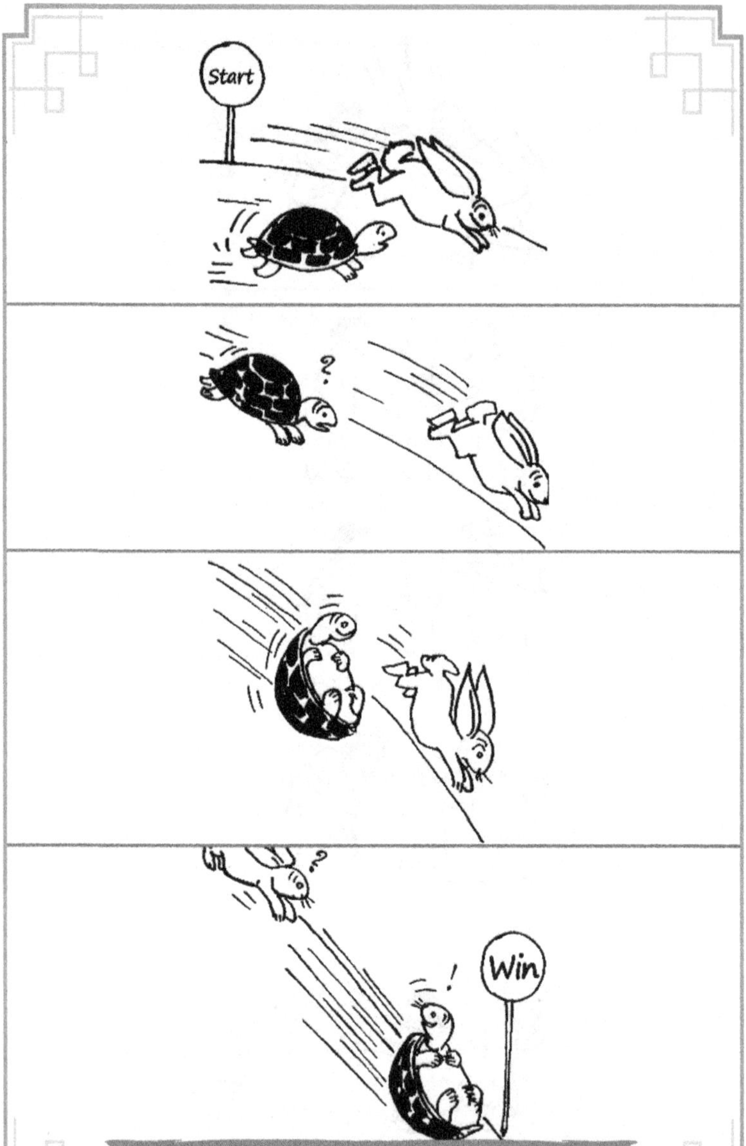

Outpace rivals by
lateral thinking.

Misjudgement embarrasses
either side.

Know whom to tell. Don't
supersede hierarchy.

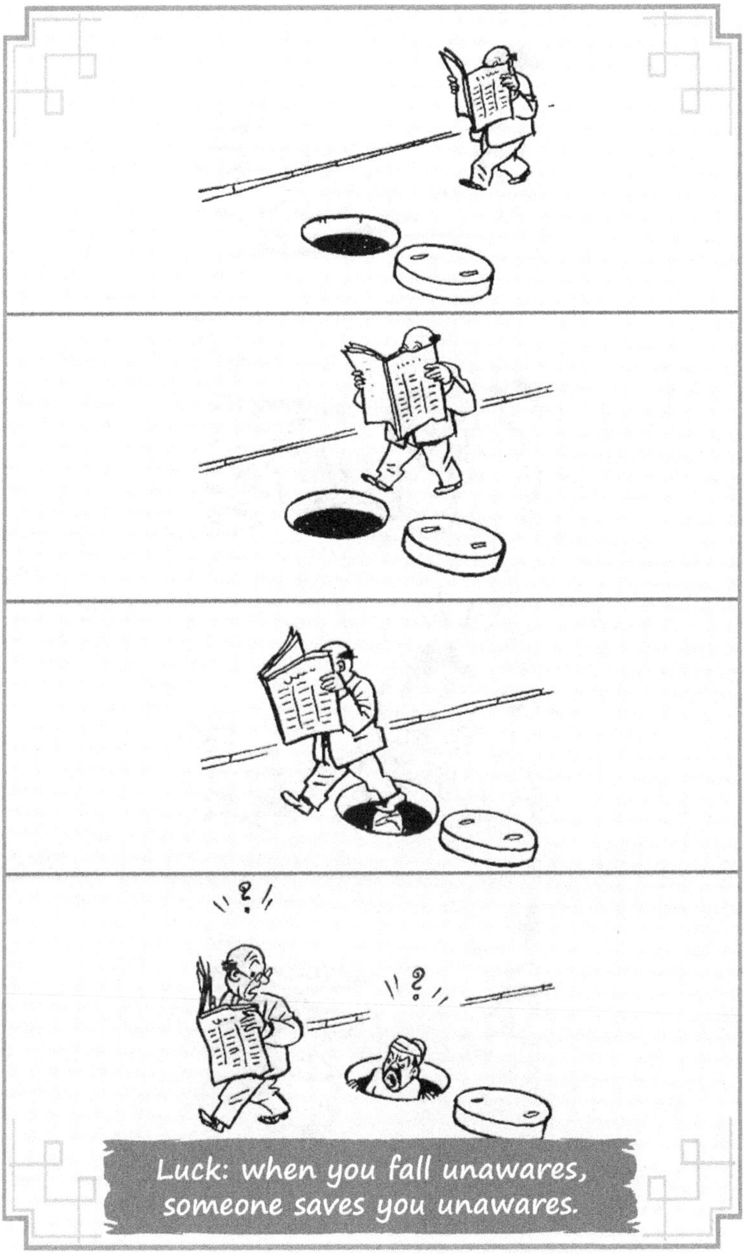

Luck: when you fall unawares,
someone saves you unawares.

Heed cautions; beware of
the hidden enemy.

School

If bundling out is
the way out, do it.

Don't be a Roman
when in Rome.

Being prenticed somewhere
does not help everywhere.

Don't follow instructions
to the letter.

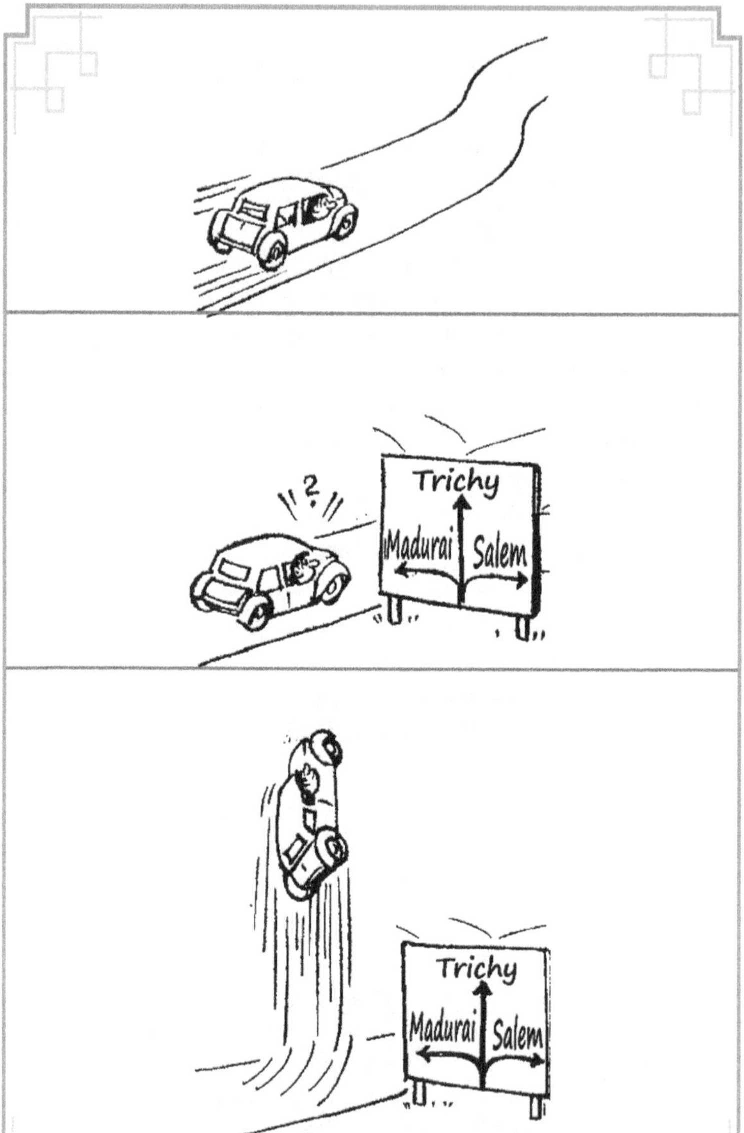

Play while you work.

Used to take to the pillion?

Oh!

So far, how many times...

Had I...

Gone...!

Bragging about experience seldom saves one.

Beware of the letter of law.

Inattention robs you
of your means.

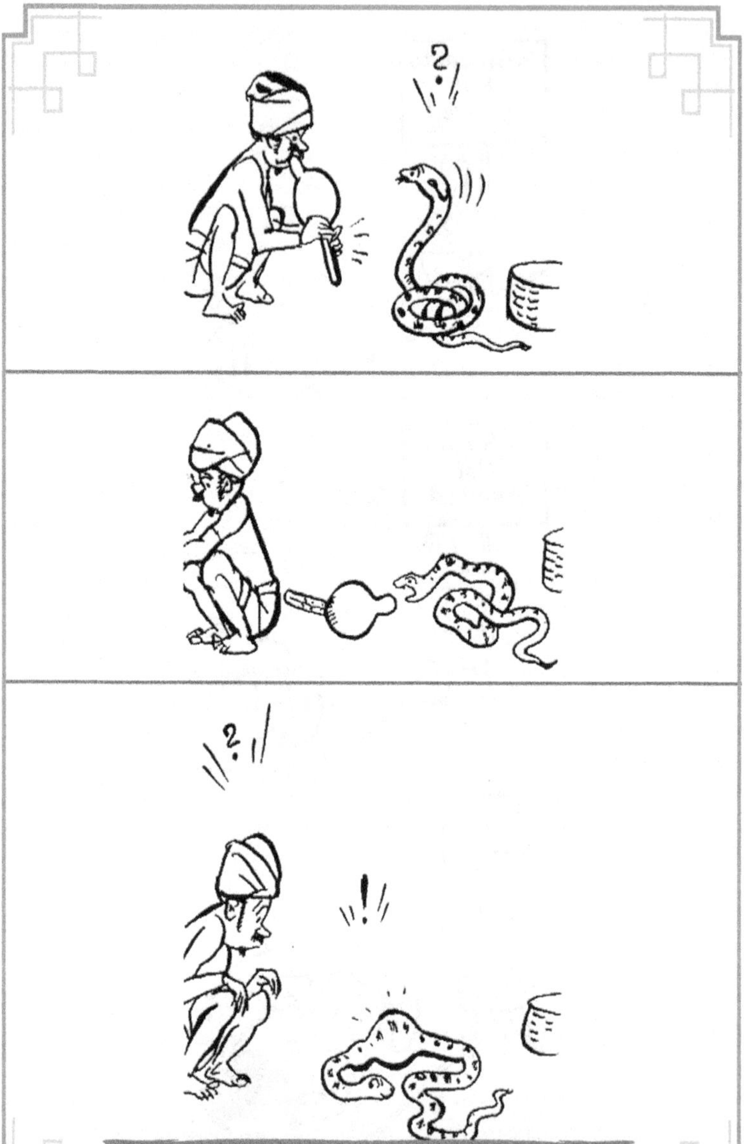

A lady hour lasts longer.

The valiant can do
even slit-rope walking.

Unexpected are the
uses of arms.

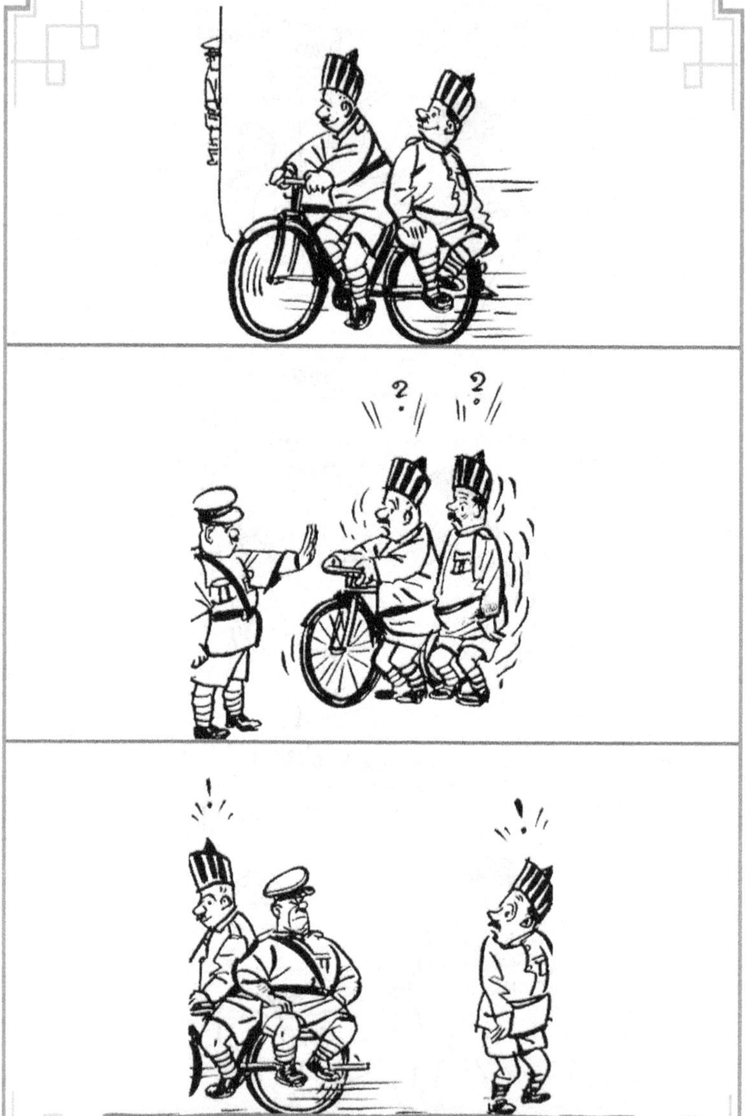

Faults or defaults,
the boss is always right.

Don't panic from afar.
Get closer to reality.

Sometimes solutions become problems.

The one who disrobes you
could re-robe you.

Visuals amuse;
words scare.

Differentiate to avoid
mistaken identity.

Age is no audacity. Adults dread what urchins dare.

Run away from one awful,
only to run into another.

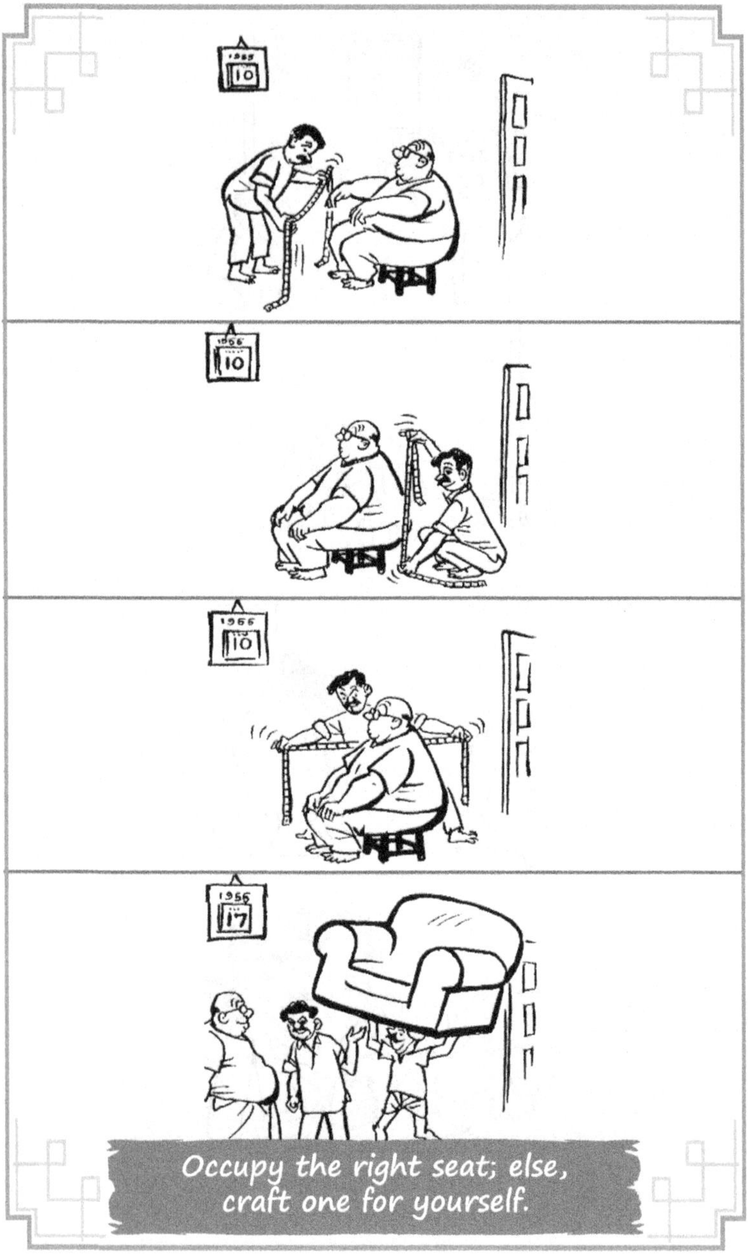

Occupy the right seat; else,
craft one for yourself.

Some gadgets work on
when you also work along.

Read the signals right!

If the shop-floor is weaker than the weakest employee, you lose.

Minions imitate bosses;
still bosses are bosses.

Wares abound; but customers
compete for one and the same.

More often you don't sense
what attracts others.

Calamities could shape one.

Phantom lies in the
eyes of the beholder.

75

Age cannot rob one's
taste for beauty.

Hunger hankers for interim relief.

1

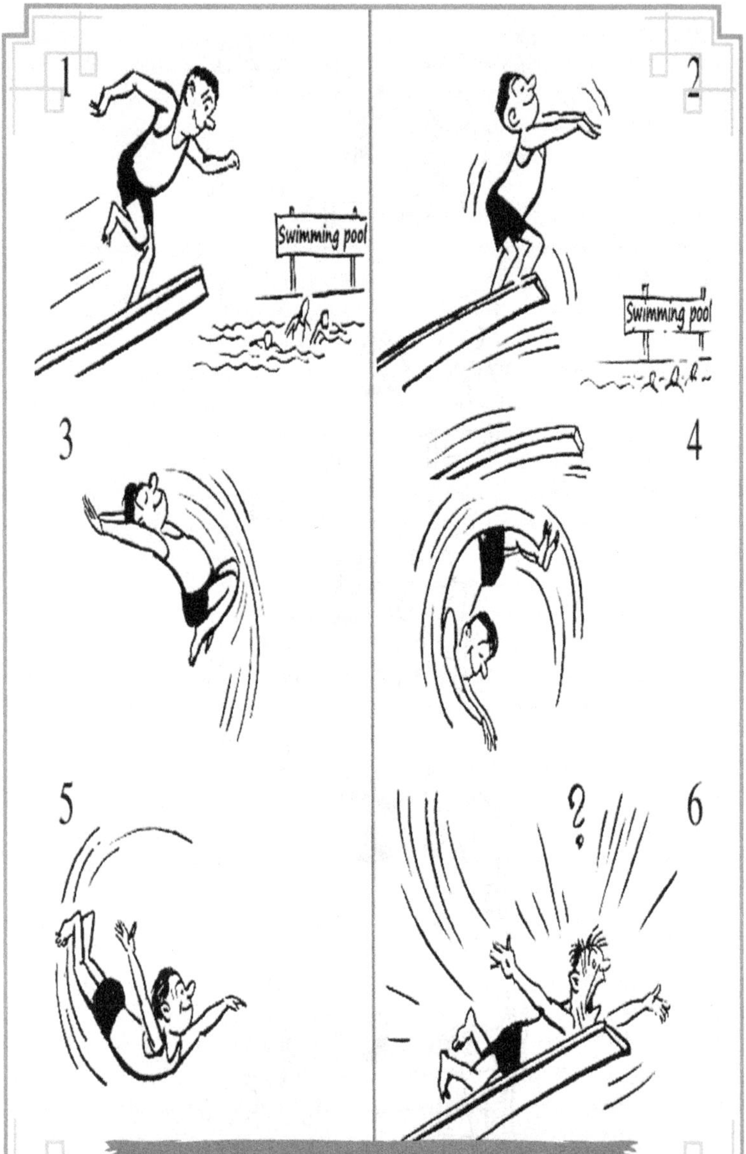

2

Swimming pool

Swimming pool

3

4

5

6

Don't overdo the preliminaries.

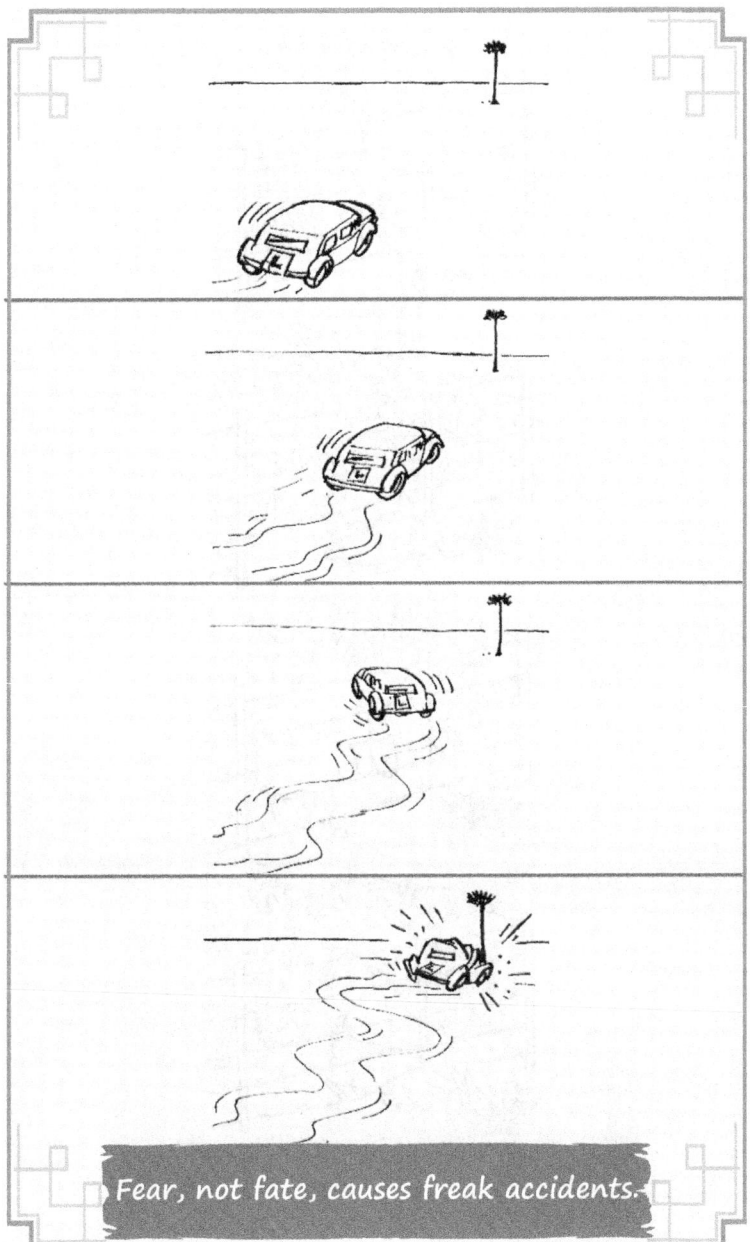

Fear, not fate, causes freak accidents.

Brave the barbs for
the acquisition route.

None buys your product
till he needs it.

1880
Music Review
Child prodigy
bright future
ahead

1900
Promising young
Muthusamy
performed
splendidly

1920
Good performance
will come to
forefront

1940
Sure to
lead in
future

1959
Muthusamy
of the afternoon
session will gain
fame shortly

**The longer the apprenticeship,
the farther the fame.**

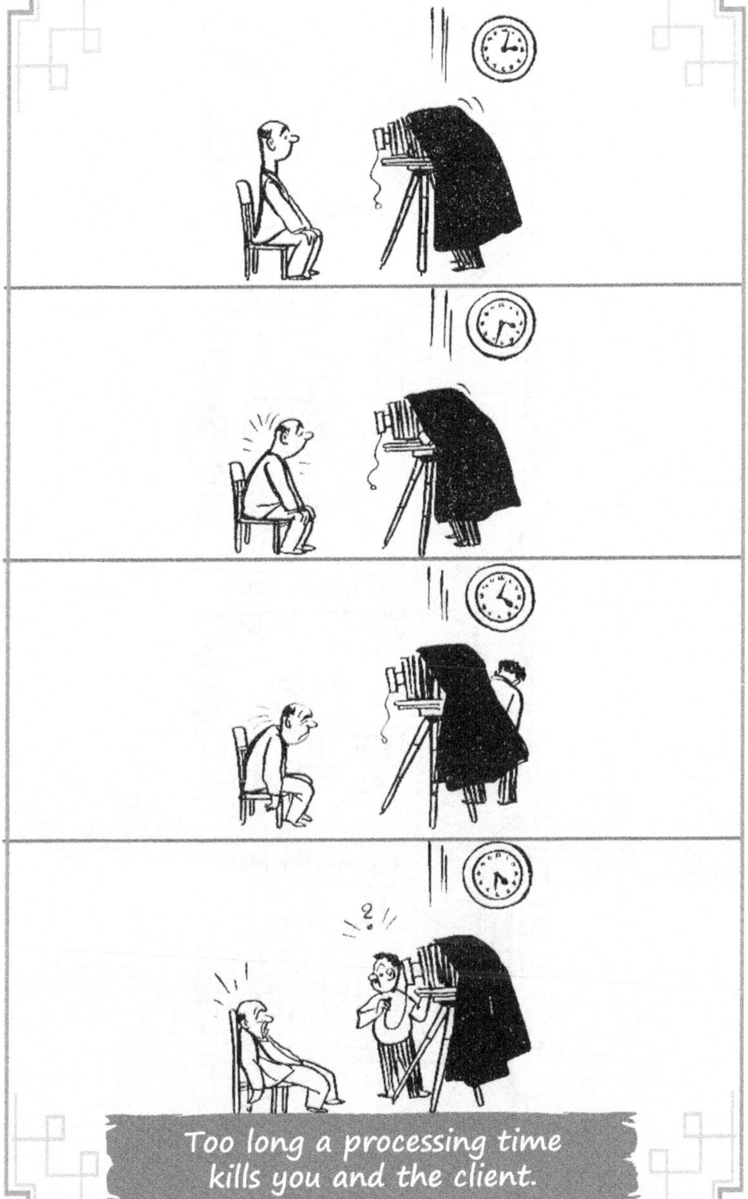

Too long a processing time
kills you and the client.

All are not customers who visit the showroom.

Manners are what you conceal.

The clever clamber by contriving their steps.

Change the methodology to avoid rebuffs.

Others do not rejoice where you do.

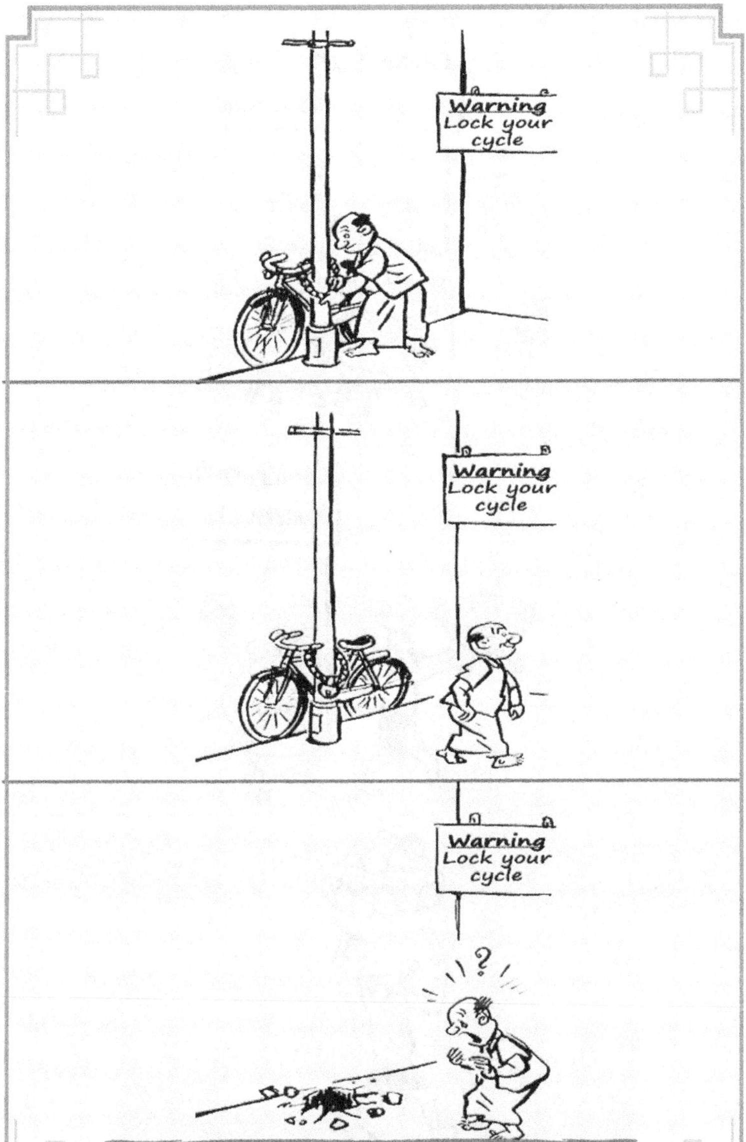

You may be uprooted where you think you are safe.

Cane Furniture
Modern Chairs Available

Cane Furnit
Modern Chai

**The user is wiser
than the maker.**

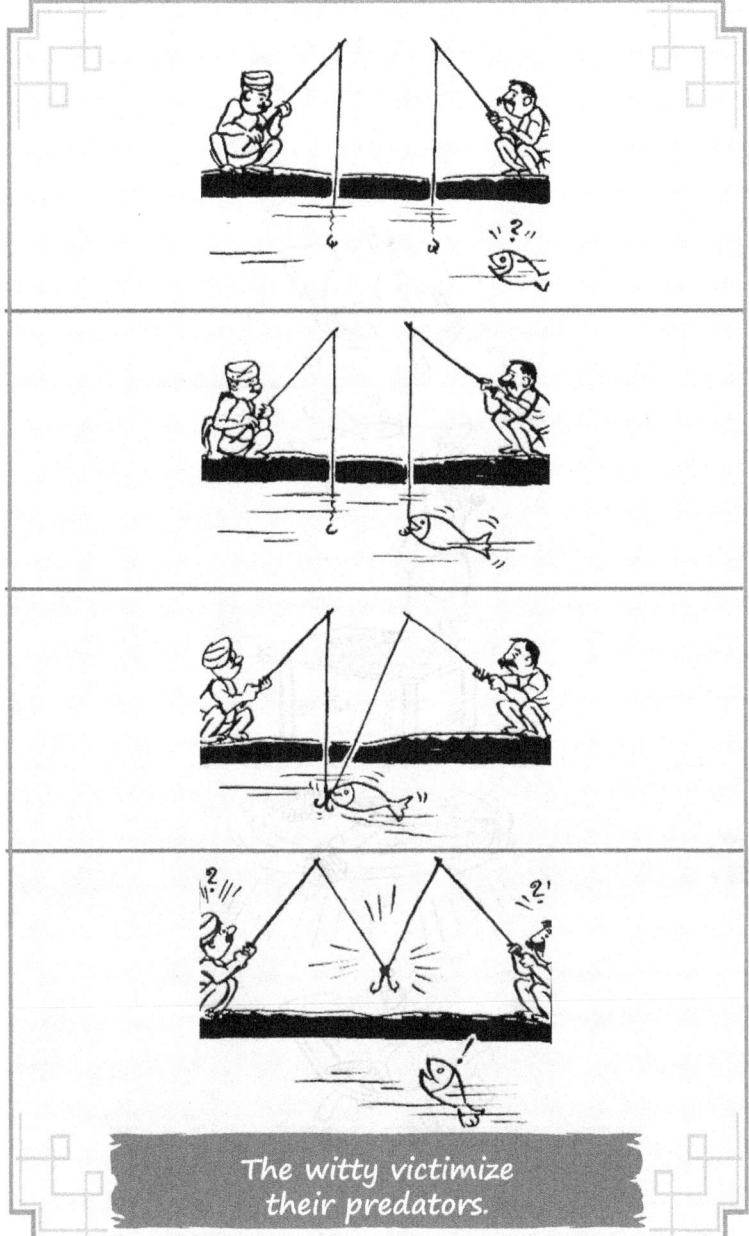

The witty victimize
their predators.

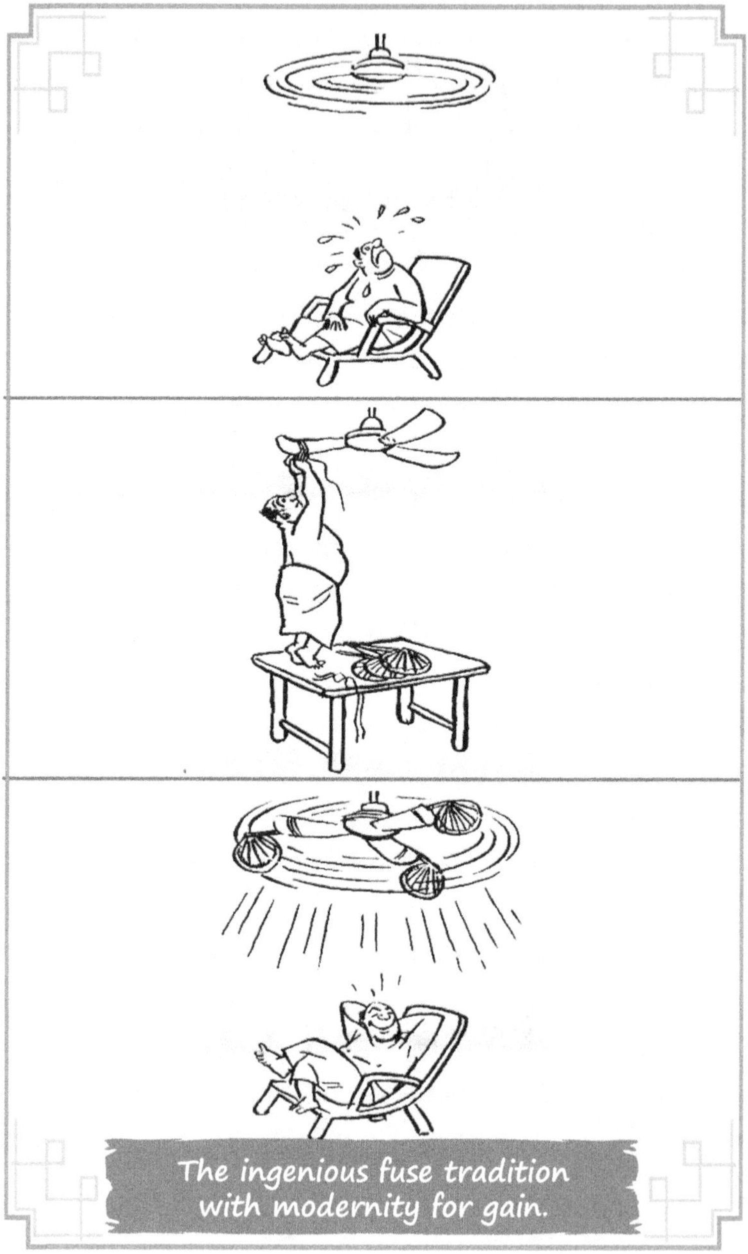

The ingenious fuse tradition with modernity for gain.

**A trap for the enemy
entraps the enemy's enemy.**

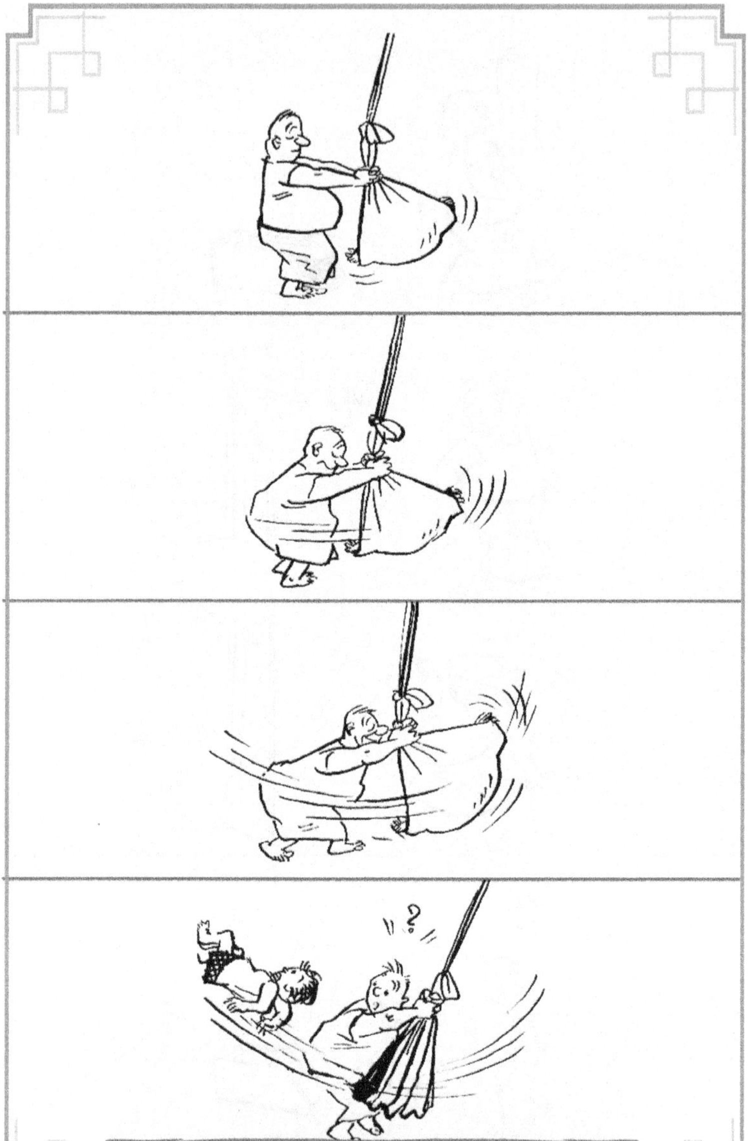

You lose what you care more.

Take before you give; that is swadharma.

Do test-marketing before launching a new product.

Beware of the enemy's enemy.

When caught, blame others.

Enjoy the fruits of your labour.

Your environ should not give misleading signals.

Wrong placement is a kill-joy.

Wait; those who retreat
might return in plenty.

Know the limit to chase
an elusive object.

The ingenious can tap
his tools from anywhere.

Health books leave one sick.

HR patronage helps
the undeserving too.

Crisis management is contriving amenities.

Don't burn permanent means
for a temporary end.

Tech-transfer helps
bend anything.

Your joy is no joy for others.

Tap child labour with the
fun of an assignment.

When resources run out,
conserve what remains.

When the original shows up,
tuck aside the look-alike.

Midway gossip robs
you of your wares.

When the brawn fails,
use the brain.

The easy route to obligation
is through the stomach.

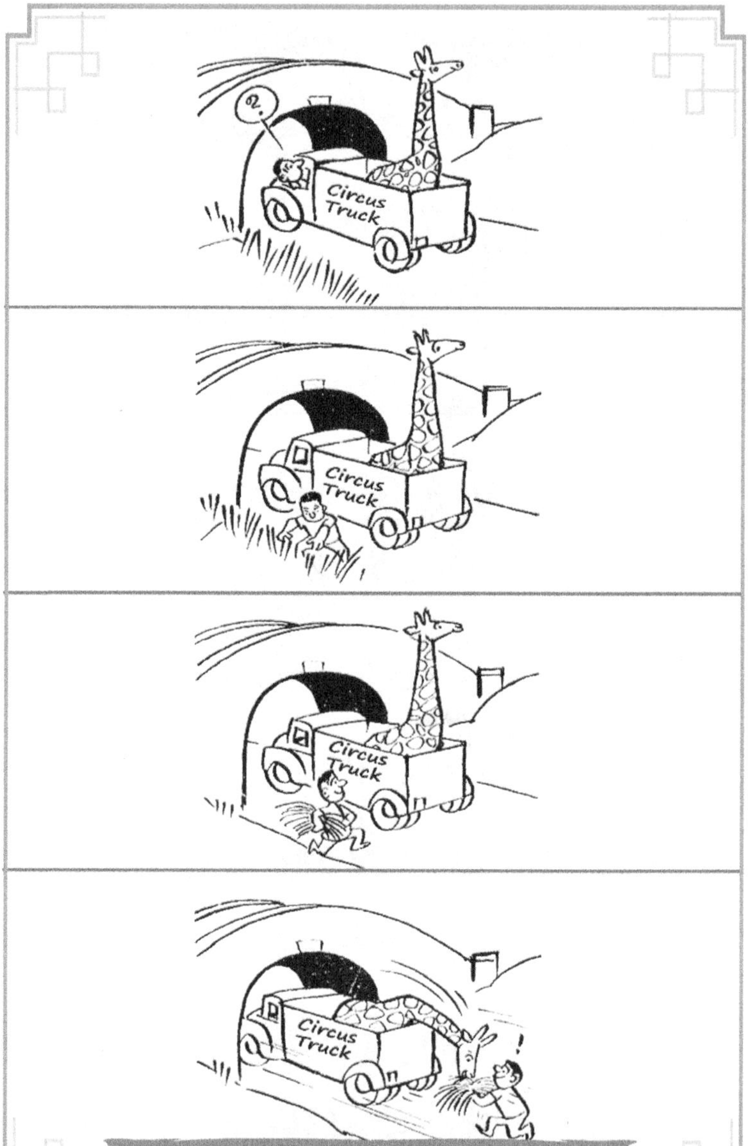

Bosses concur; but aides clash,
to the peril of the bosses.

Shed inhibitions: Look
beyond and cheer up.

Photo Studio

Photo Studio

Monks too need mundane props.

At times wrong pointers
leave the right message.

Wares beckon customers.

Natural Curtain...
Fresh, Fragrant....

Natural Curtain...
Fresh, Fragrant....

**Demonstrate yourself
the user-friendliness.**

Hostility transcends!

Redress the first punishment
with the second.

Please the dissenters and proceed.

Open door policy is welcome, but irksome;
you have to open the backdoor for relief.

Shop-lifters can come in any form.

Dislocation
Treatment

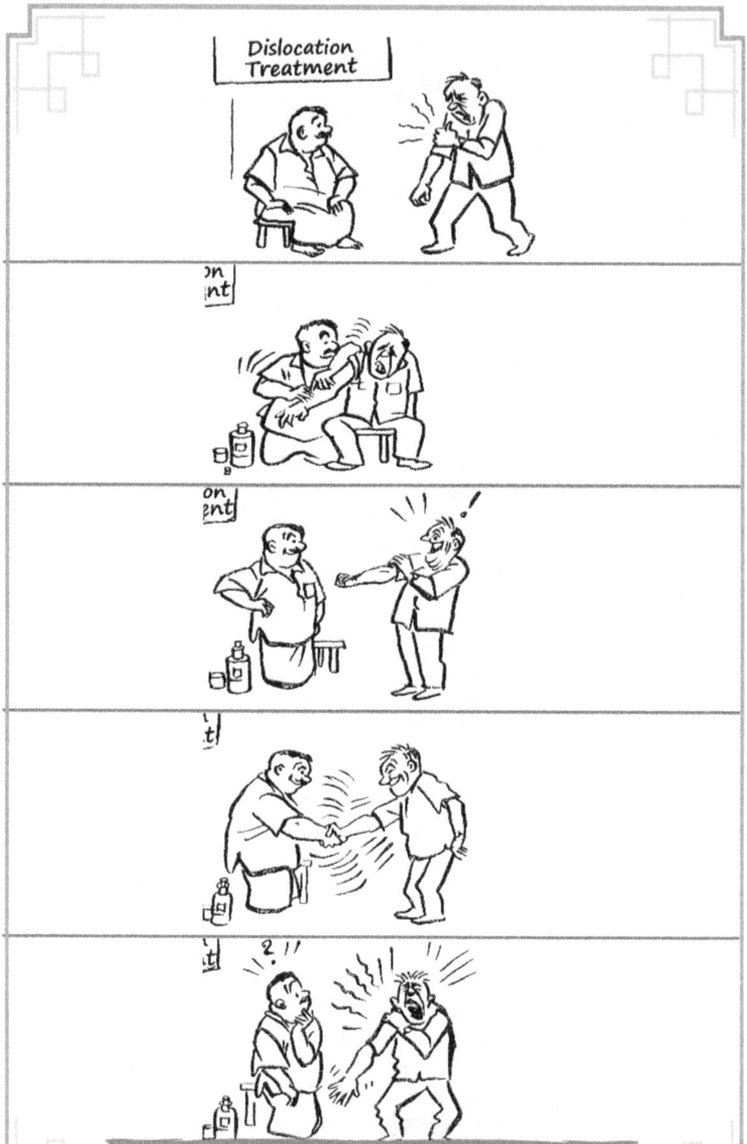

Once the business is over,
quit the spot for good.

Pittance of a gift rebounds
on your face.

Names justify things irksomely.

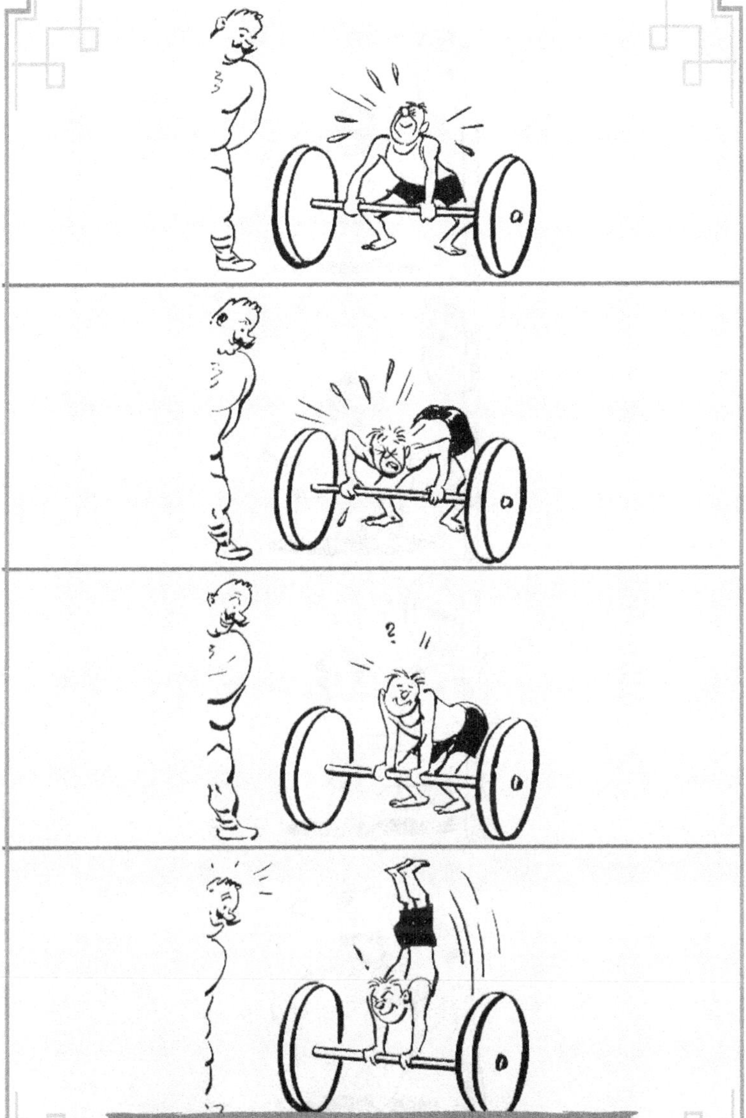

When you cannot outdo
others, just outwit them.

Be strong enough to bend
anything to your advantage.

Rats smell men before
men smell rats.

Management: Say it with fun

**Possessing is not happiness;
but seeing it is!**

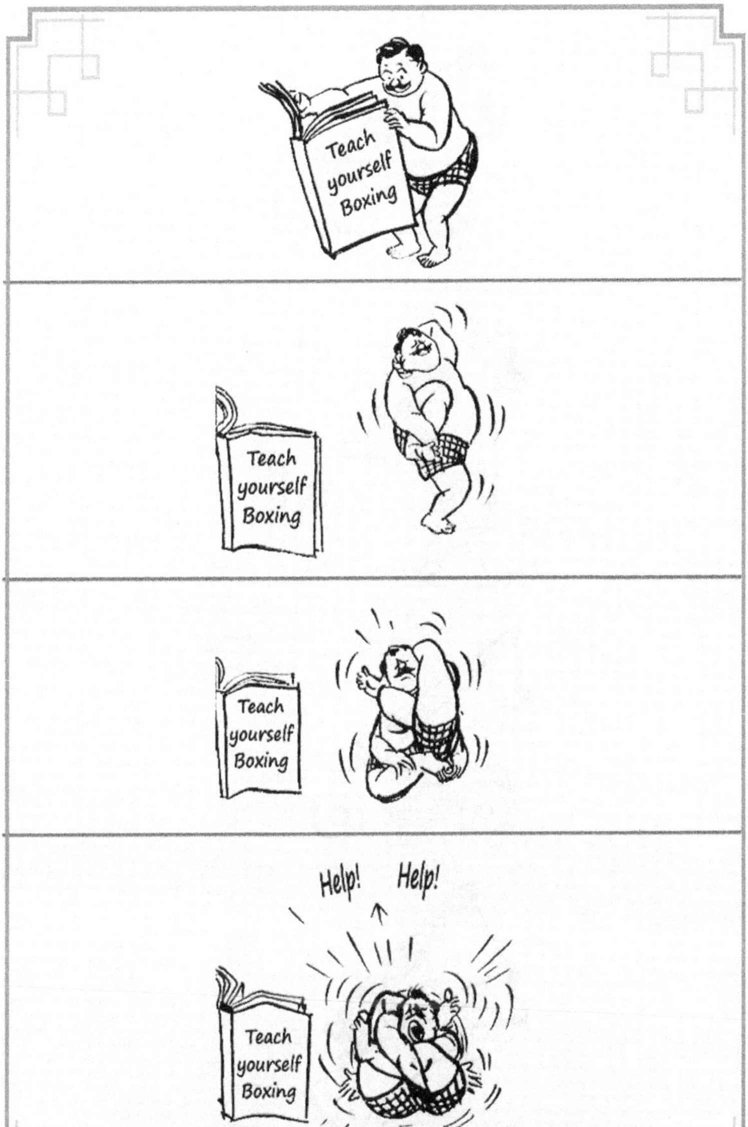

Distance education is
distress education.

Tut Sss

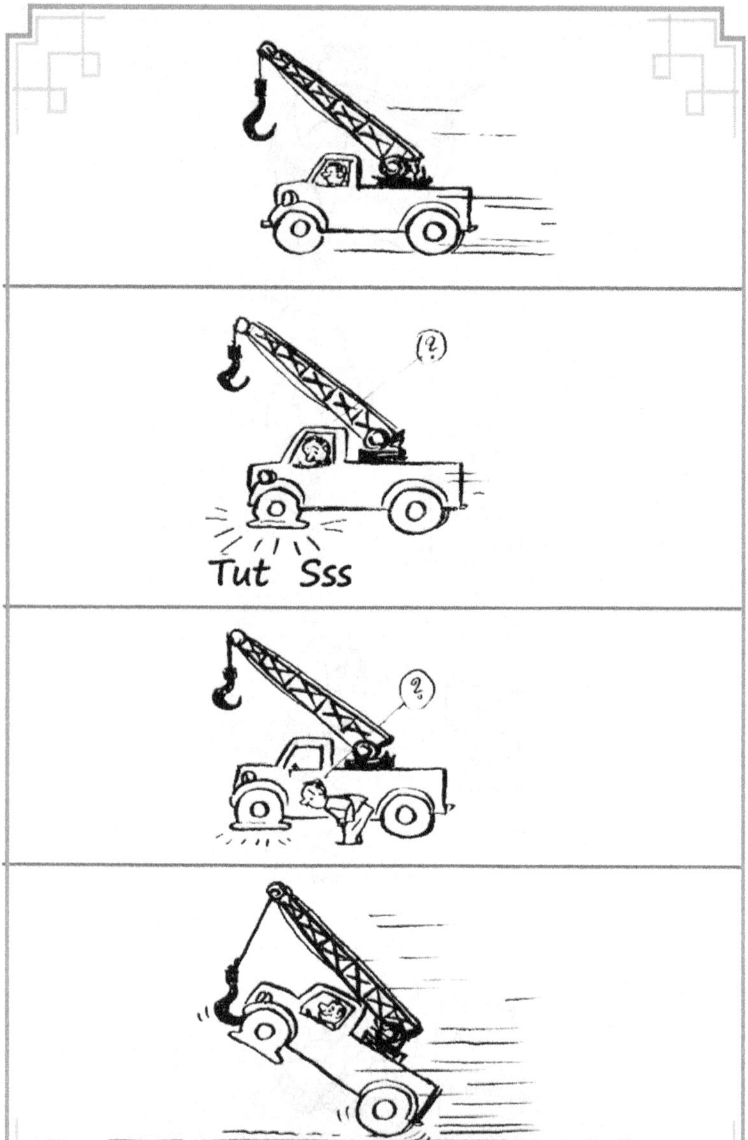

Crisis management calls for
tapping internal resources.

Spot decision helps save time, money and agony.

A donkey is a donkey
wherever it is!

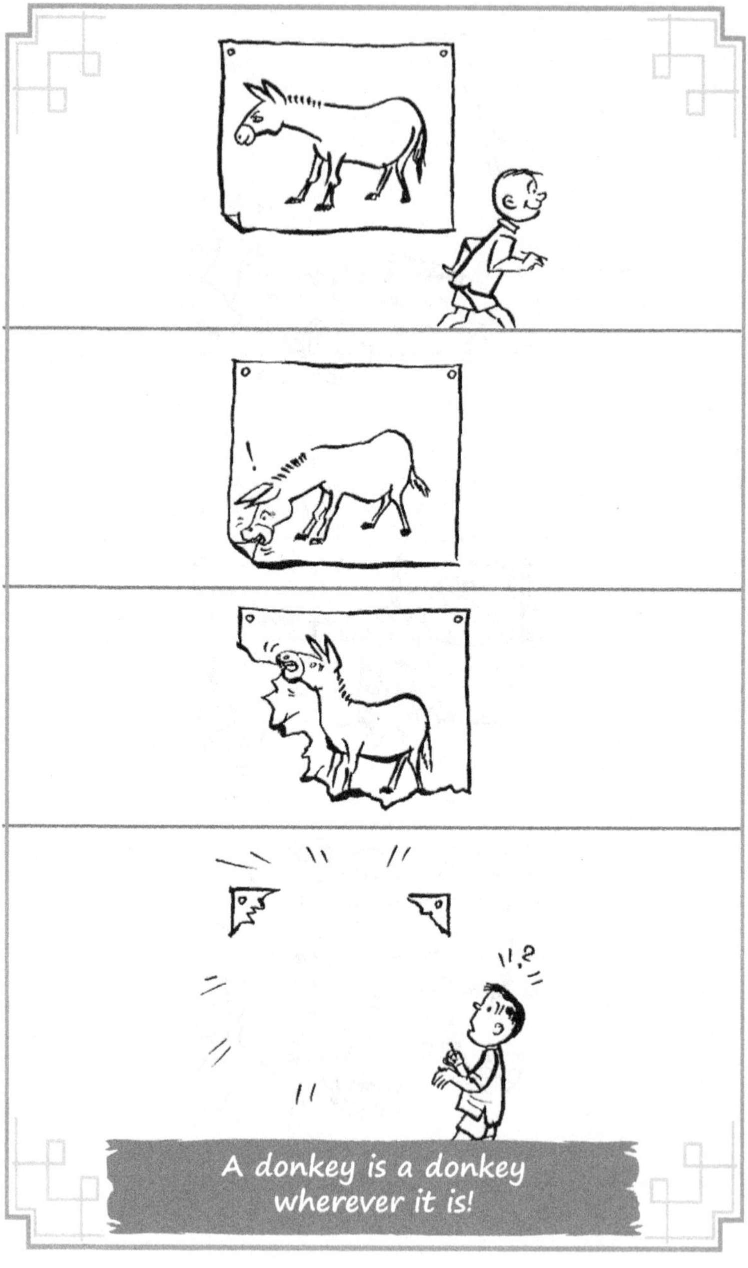

Reminders stare in any form;
respond with alacrity.

The clever hitch-hike
with their vehicles.

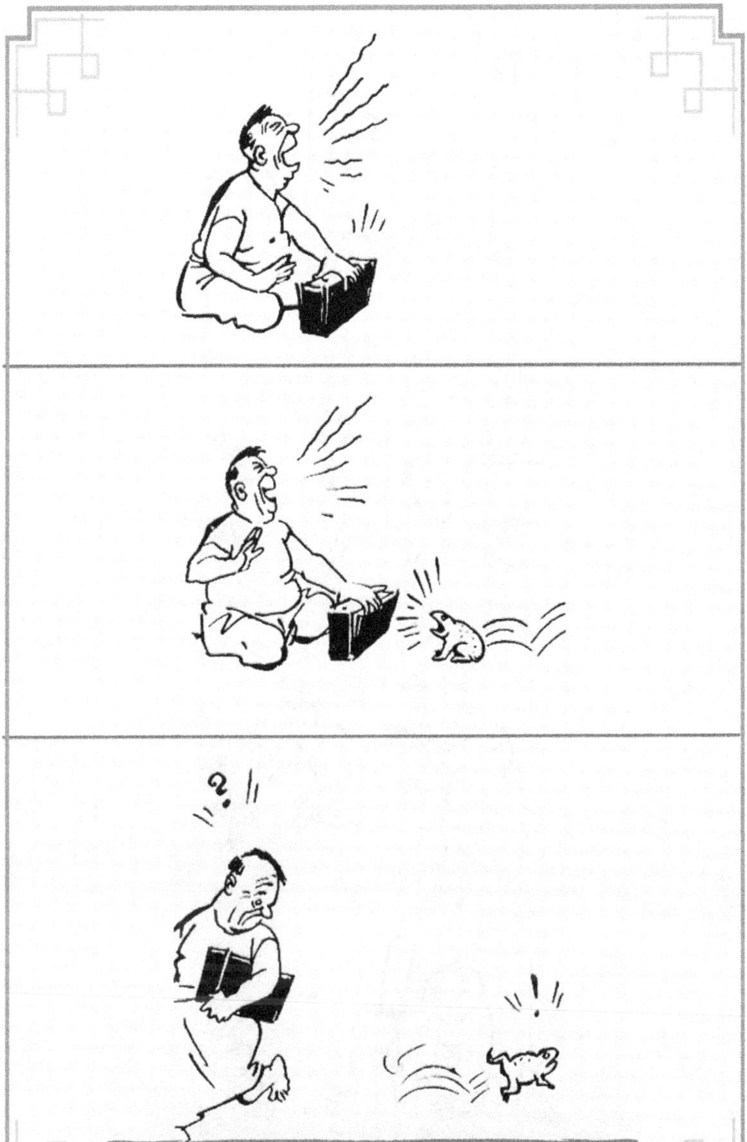

Fold up, when you face savvy critics.

Take to heels when
your tricks get exposed.

Head weight helps,
if it can keep you cool.

Customer preferences could baffle you.

Fuss of a focus
hits off the mark.

Be a monkey to
shoot a monkey!

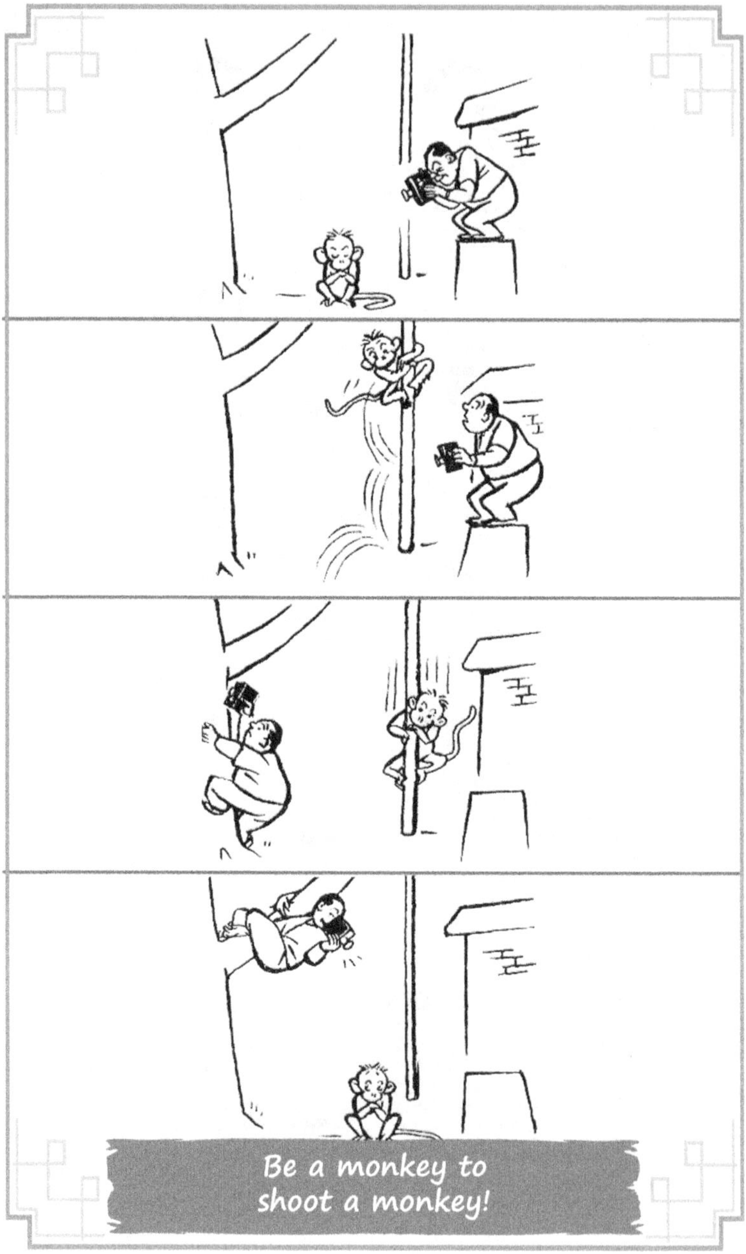

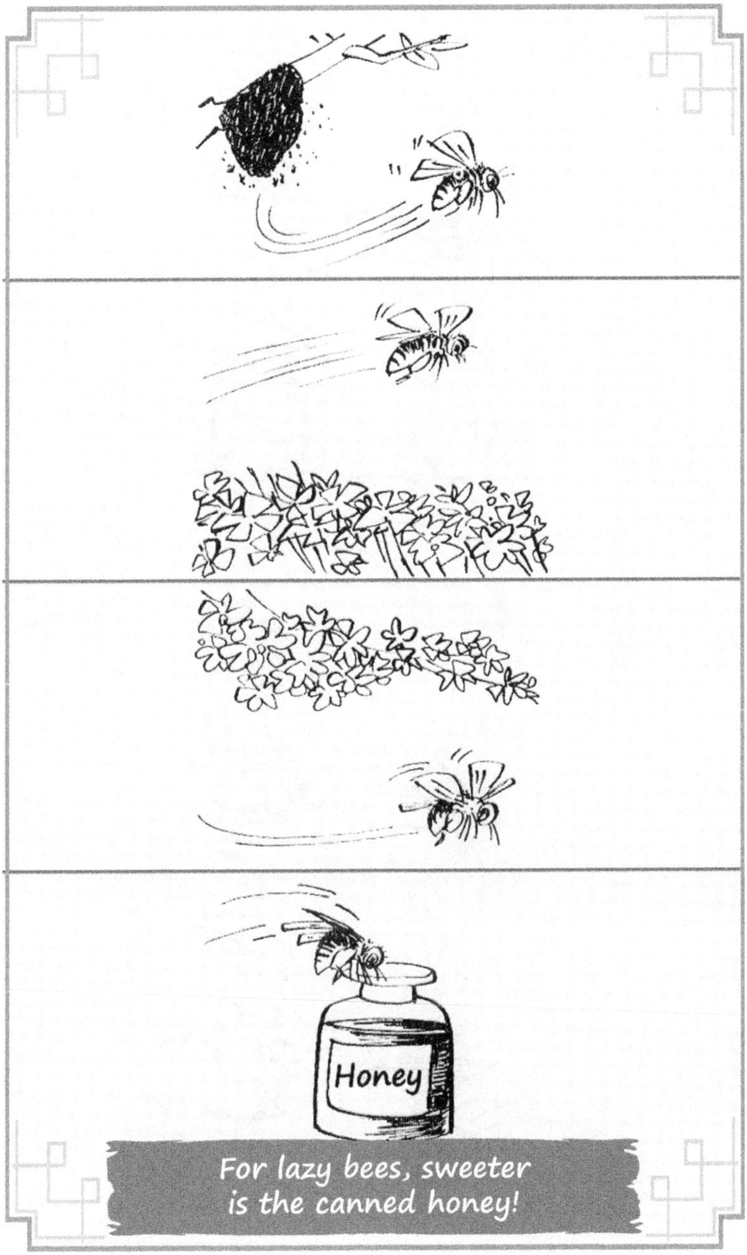

For lazy bees, sweeter
is the canned honey!

Man snares, God saves.

Hurt? Put on cheers and seek help.

Echo Hill

Hello, this is Ramasamy.

Echo Hill

Hello, this is Ramasamy.

Echo Hill

It is 8.30 now

Echo Hill

It is 8.31 now

Echoes are more than exact.

Complete your task and earn fame.

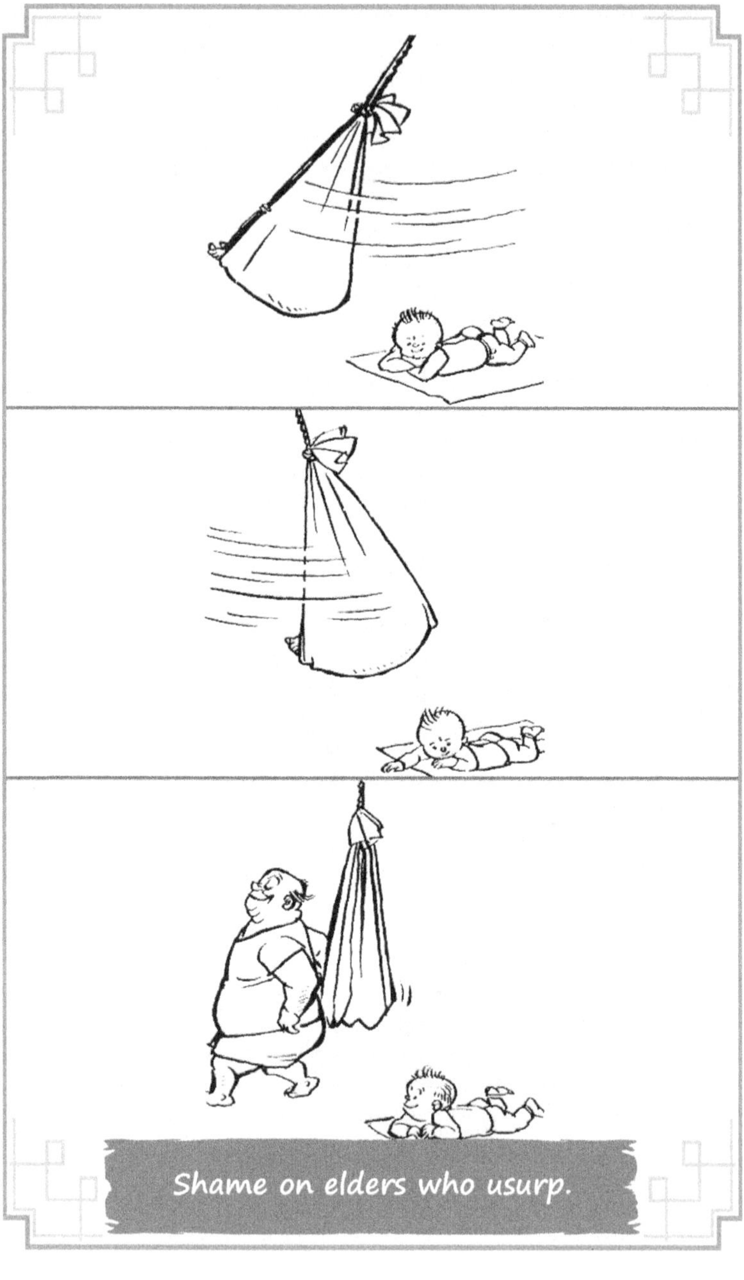

Shame on elders who usurp.

Help is havoc when
a stranger butts in.

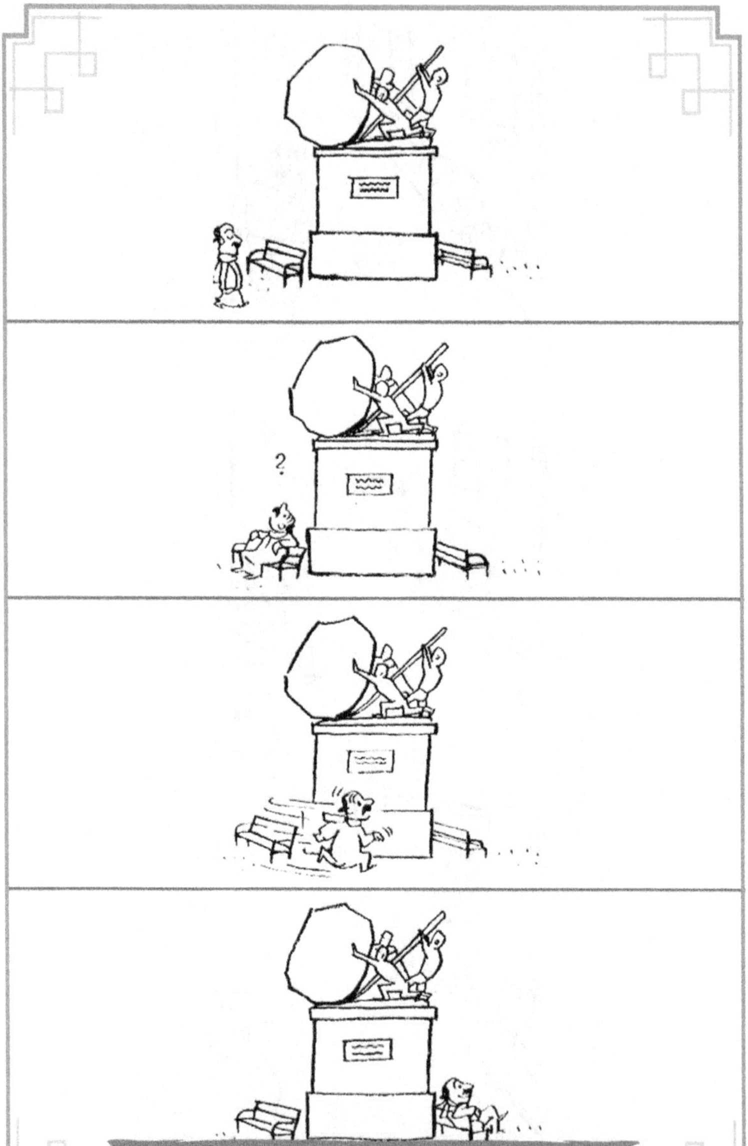

The weak dread
non-existent dangers.

Self-interest peps up all
calculations and applications.

Each covers up without
the other knowing it.

No gain without
a loss somewhere.

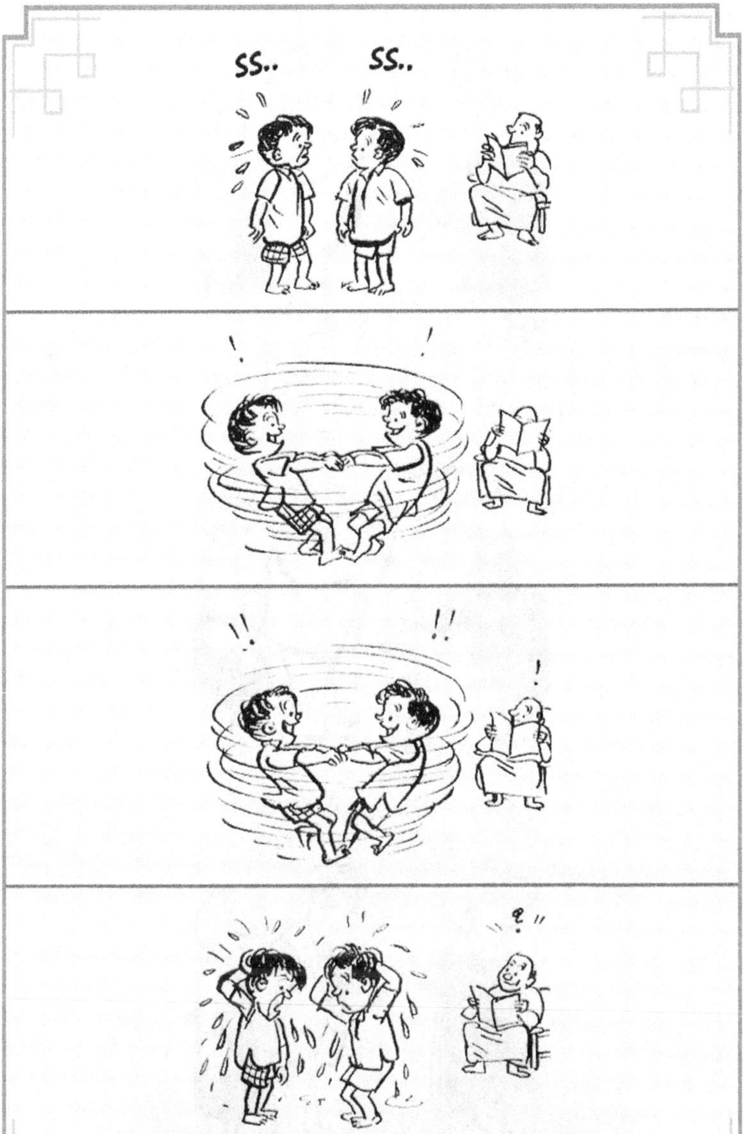

SS.. SS..

Relaxing also leads to sweating.

Wait for the response of others.

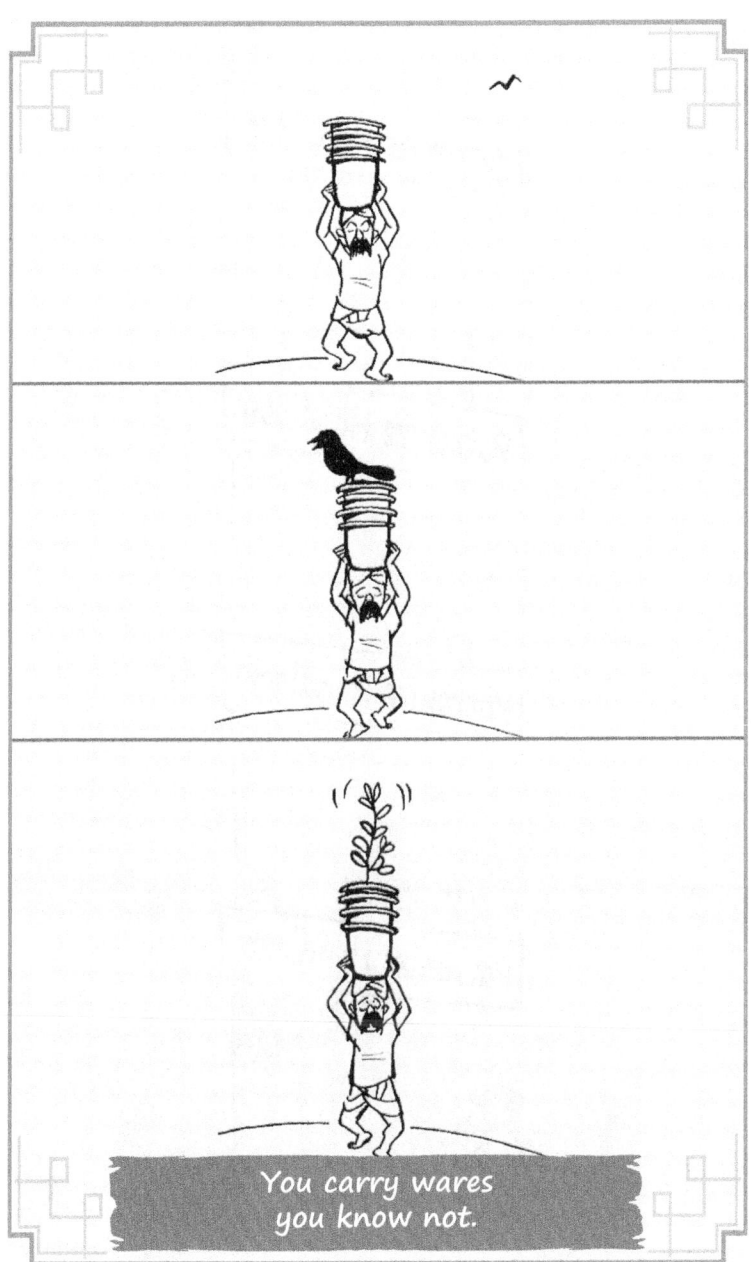

You carry wares
you know not.

Patronize Handloom

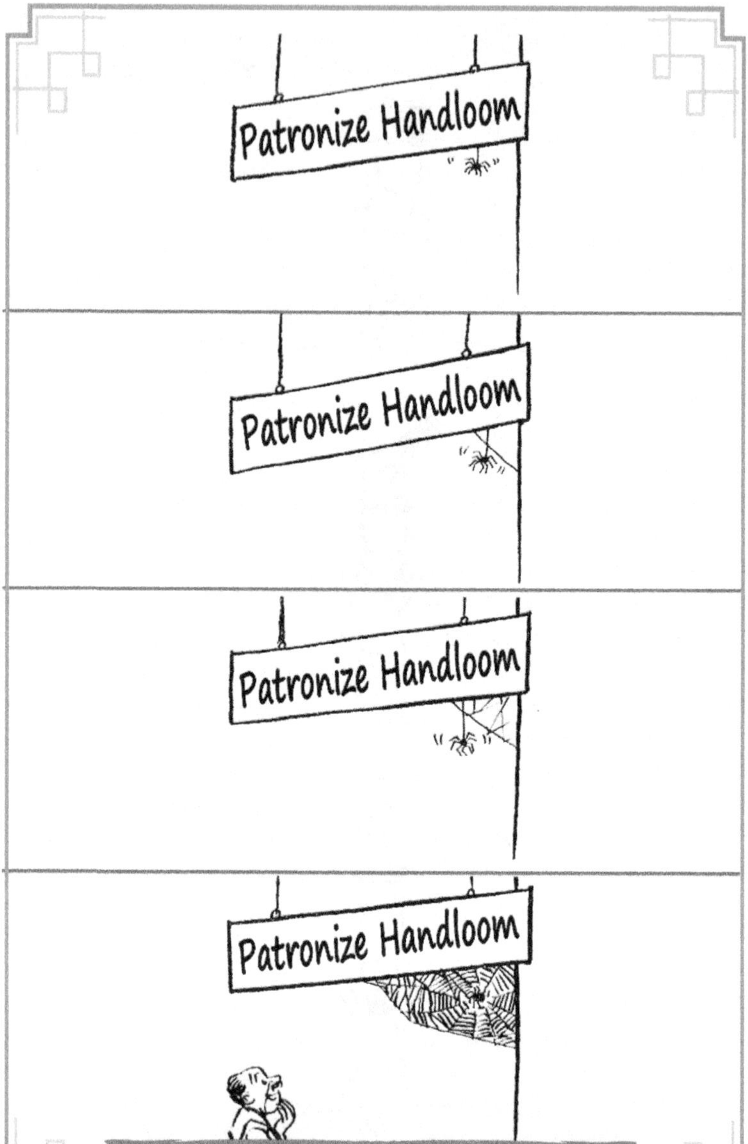

Patronize Handloom

Patronize Handloom

Patronize Handloom

**Those who talk are lazy;
those who don't are busy.**

Improvise for ease
and better results.

Daring performances are deceptive.

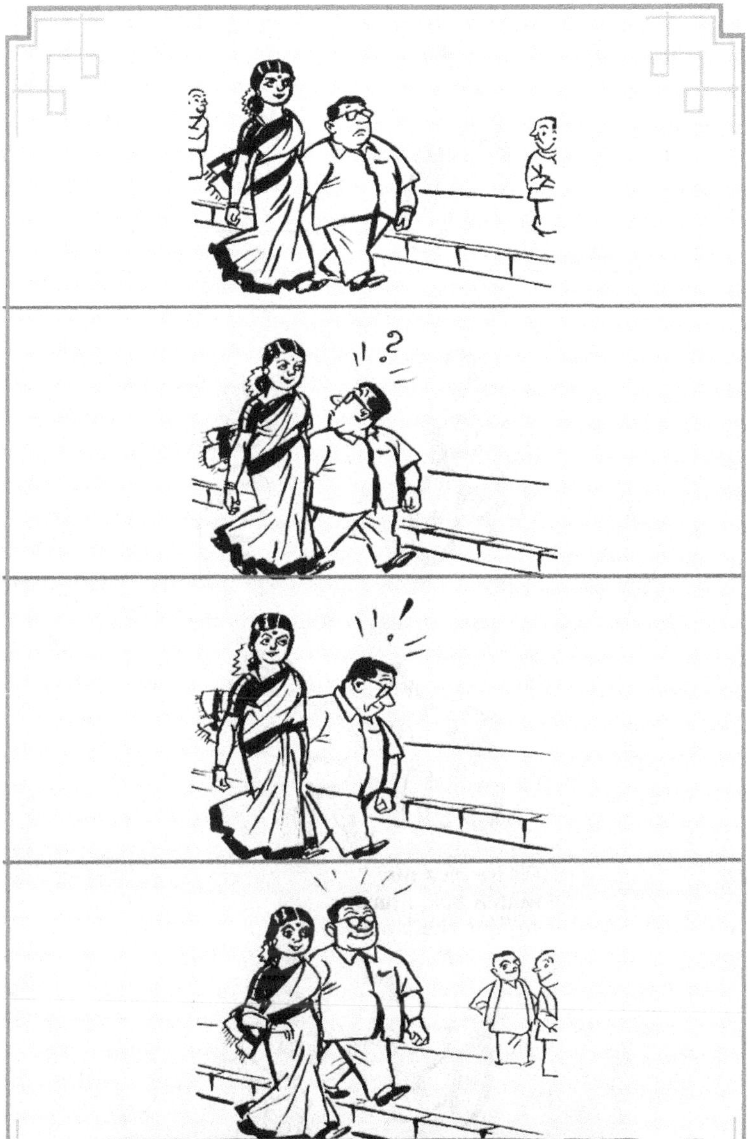

When possible, measure
up to the partner.

Please give me
match box. I have
to light the lamp.
↑

Outwit law by
feigning to follow it.

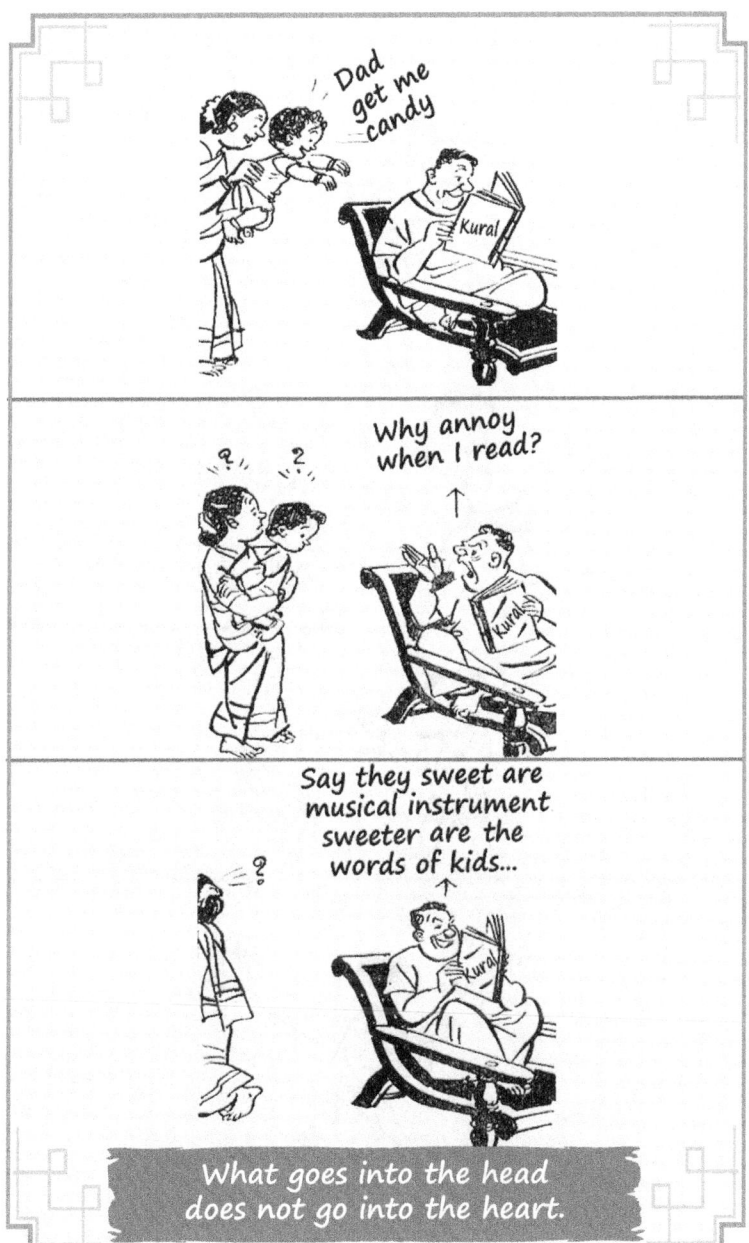

What goes into the head
does not go into the heart.

The clever never run out of resources.

Return to walking for health,
after hunting for wealth.

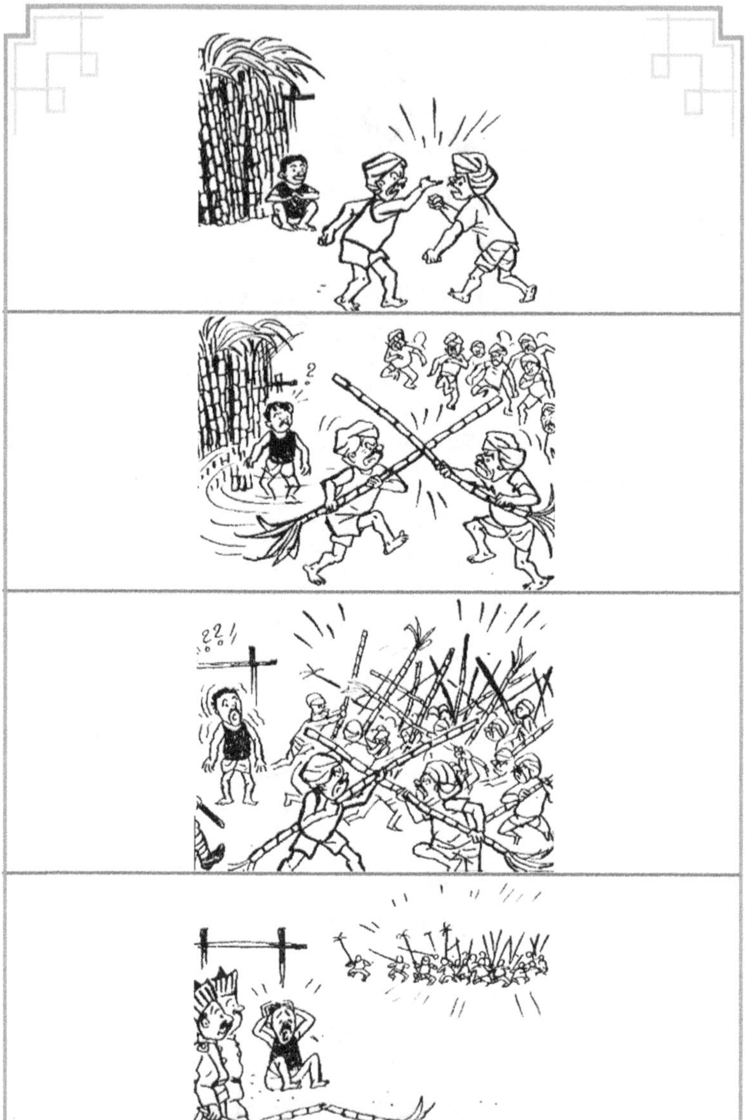

What to sell apart,
mind where you sell.

When a partner flees out of
fear, draw him to safety.

Ills rebound.

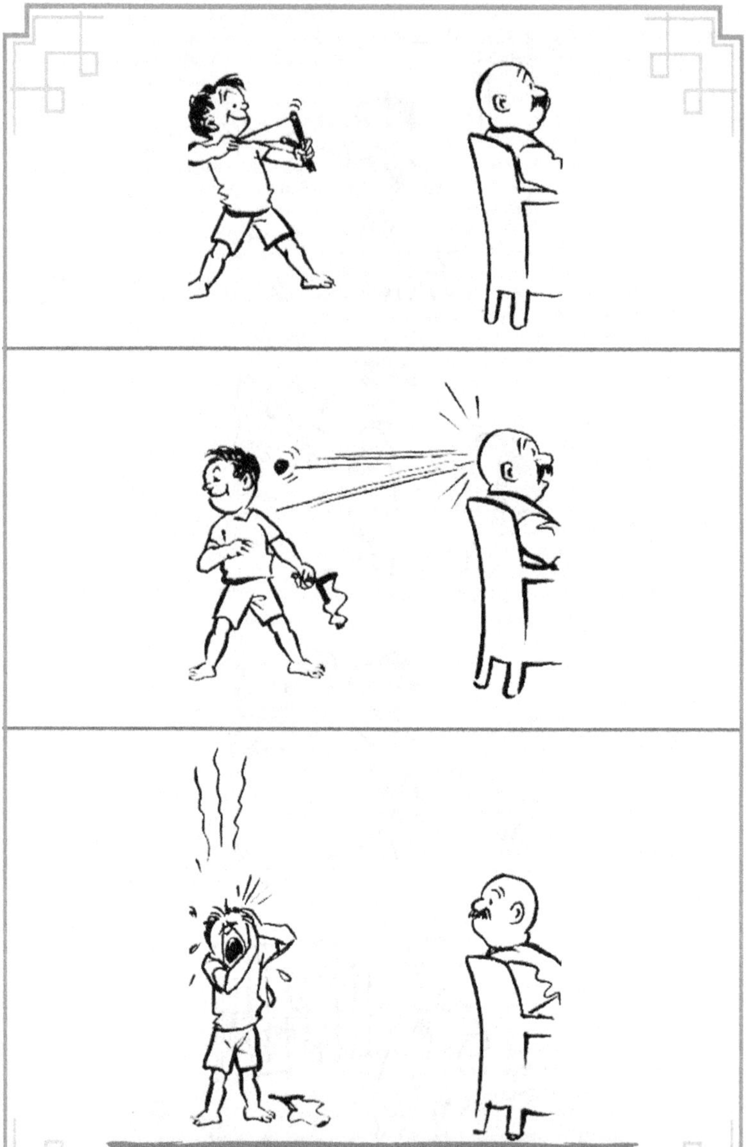

Innovation helps you relax,
even as you work.

Probe the calm
behind the storm.

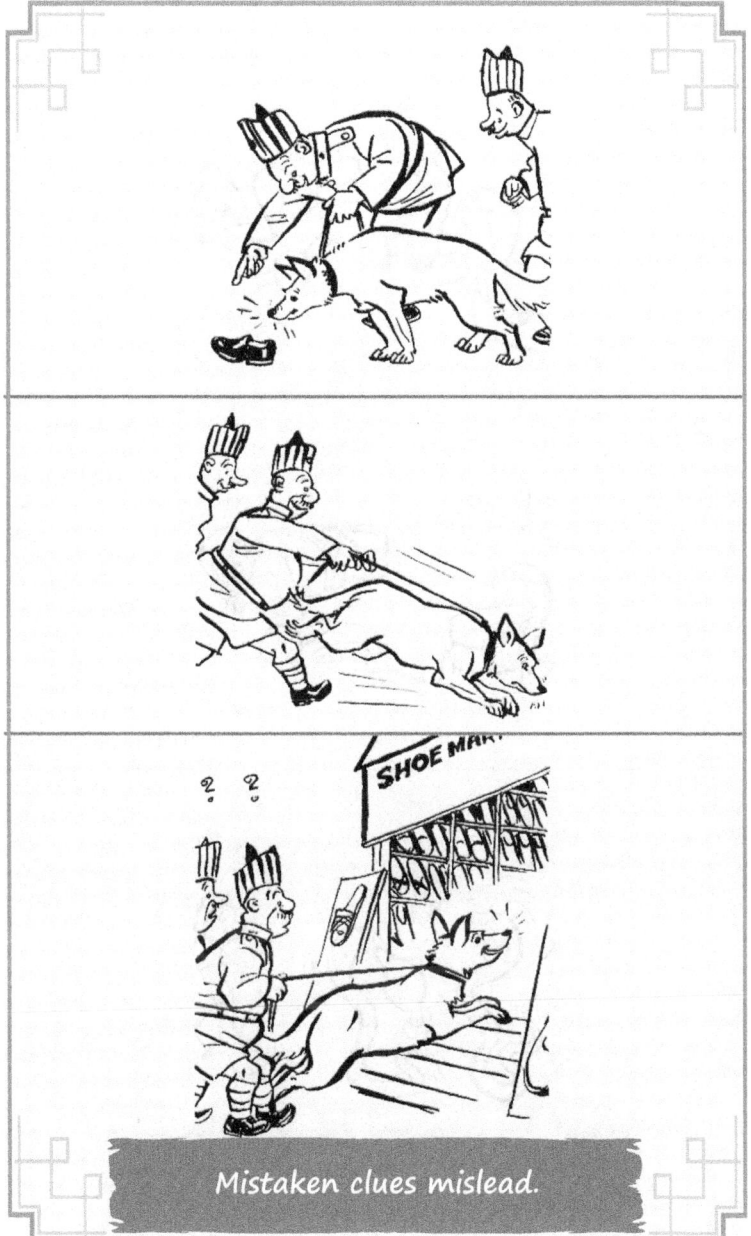

Mistaken clues mislead.

When the boss sleeps,
the minions play.

You don't feel the heat
till you are told.

Capacity expansion
can come in any form.

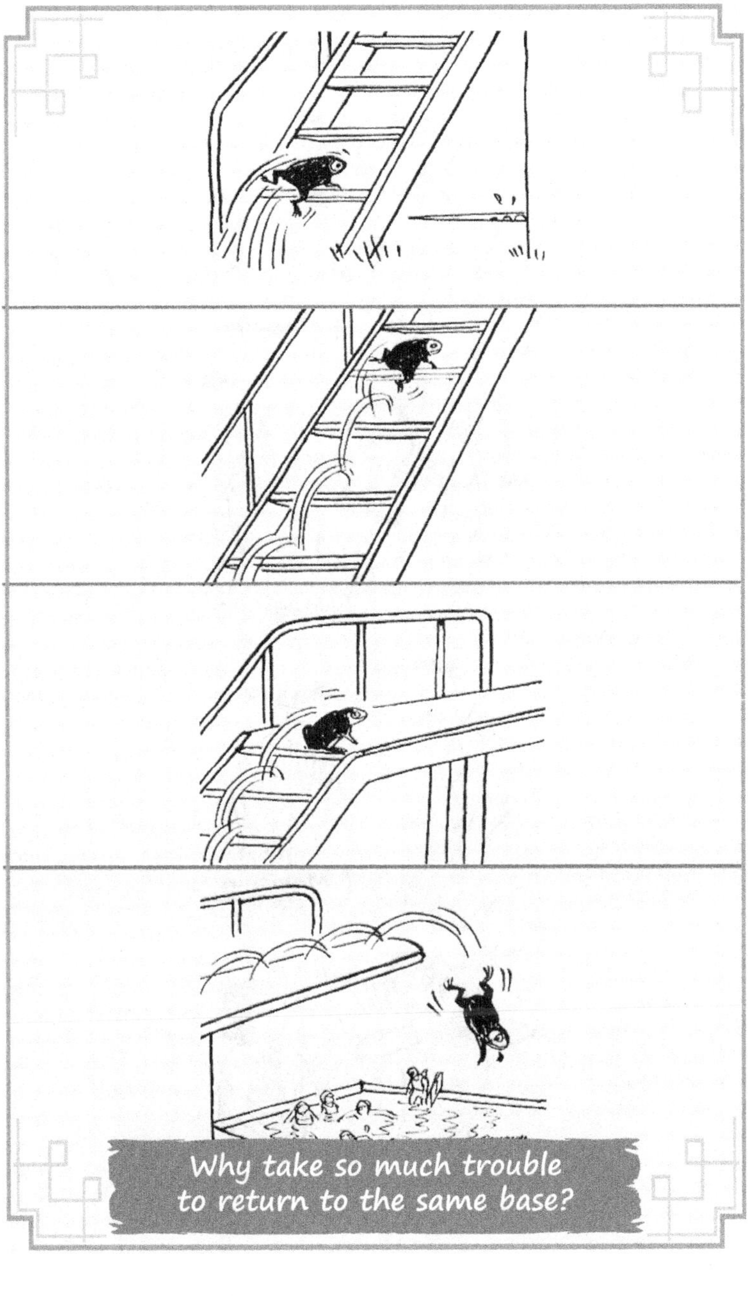

Why take so much trouble
to return to the same base?

Magician

Magician

Magician

Magician

Pill is mightier
than the sword.

Anyone is a Romeo
before a Juliet.

Cry for attention at the right place.

Armours embolden cowards.

Modernisation does not always pay.

Ingenuity cuts
through hindrances.

People take lessons
in their own way.

Zoo - Reptiles

Snake varieties

Zoo

Hose

Illusions are scary; be wary.

Be in the right company;
mind your age.

The spark of originality is
fusing fun with utility.

Be a professional
in everything.

Don't misread market
reports and panic.

**Location matters. Beach
is no place for speech.**

Tax disrobes!

Patience personified
is no sign of growth.

The ward uncared for
goes elsewhere.

If you cannot outrun,
disengage the wares and settle.

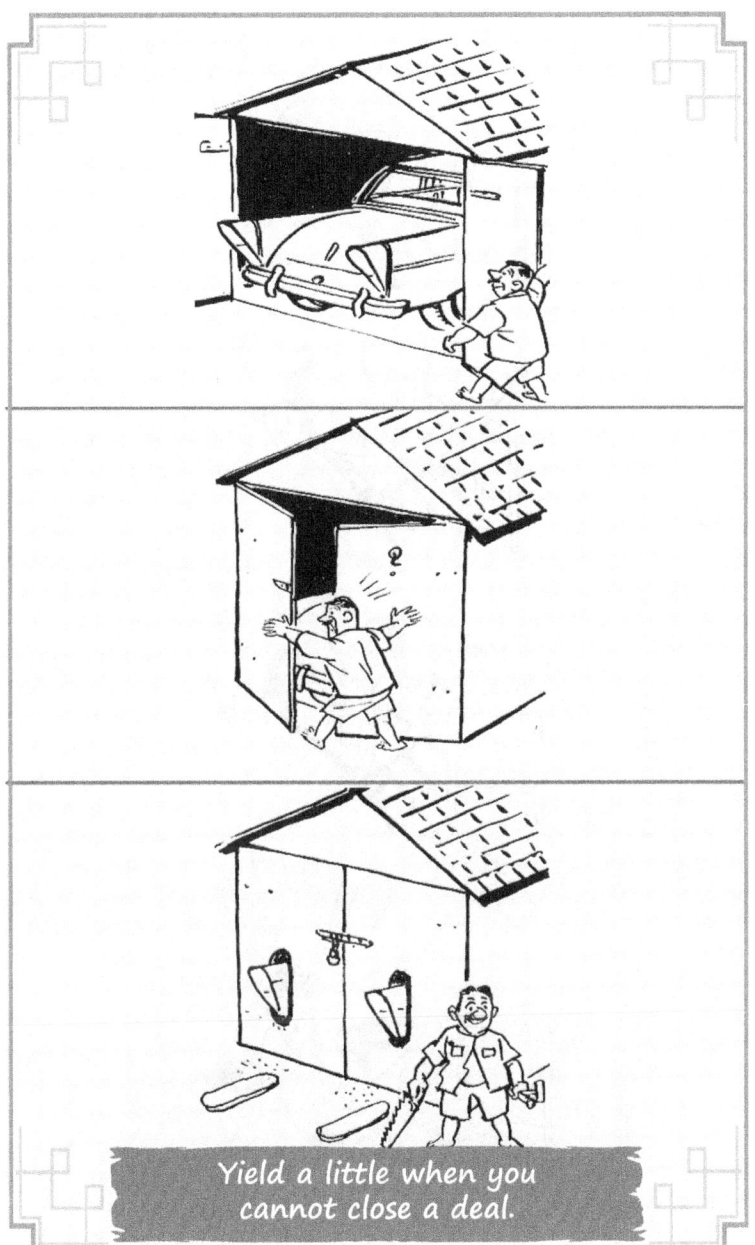

Yield a little when you
cannot close a deal.

Fancy is safe if
the footing is firm.

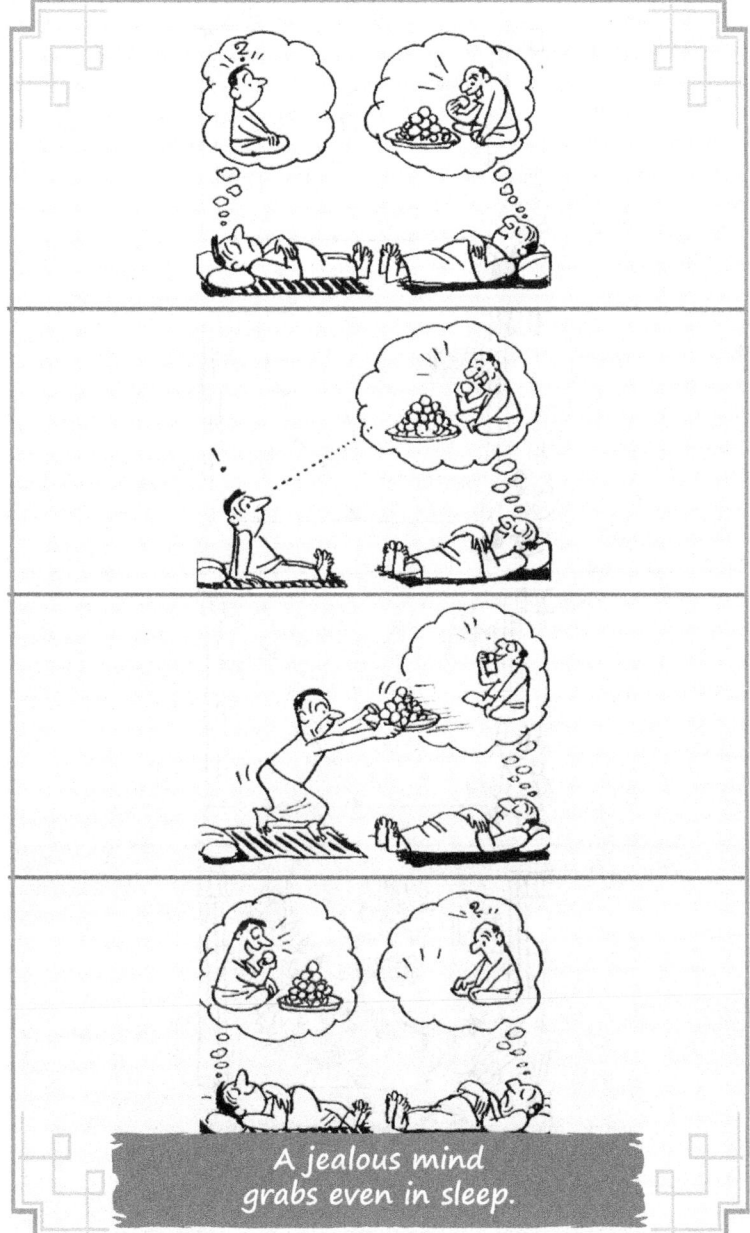

A jealous mind
grabs even in sleep.

The clever turn their
liabilities into assets.

Changing place is not
changing direction.

Sculptor

Sculptor

Sculptor

Sculpture Show

Rock

You can slap a raw deal on
ill-informed customers.

Know what to chase
to avoid risks.

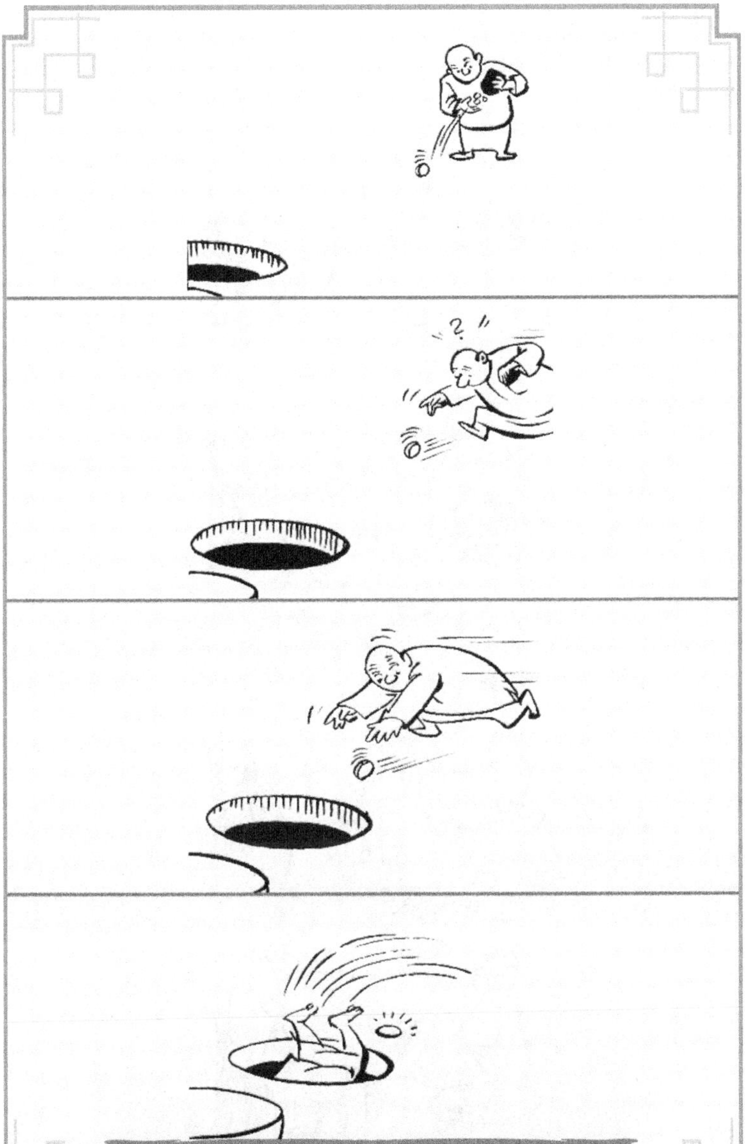

More legs do not mean
a more capacious mouth.

Ladders help the unexpected.

All is not big that looks big.

Disorder is the order of kids.

Don't poke your nose
too deep into anything.

Goods are fine in showrooms.

You don't find takers
where you are harsh.

Sometimes weapons are
bigger than the enemies.

Phrase your signboards
without ambiguity.

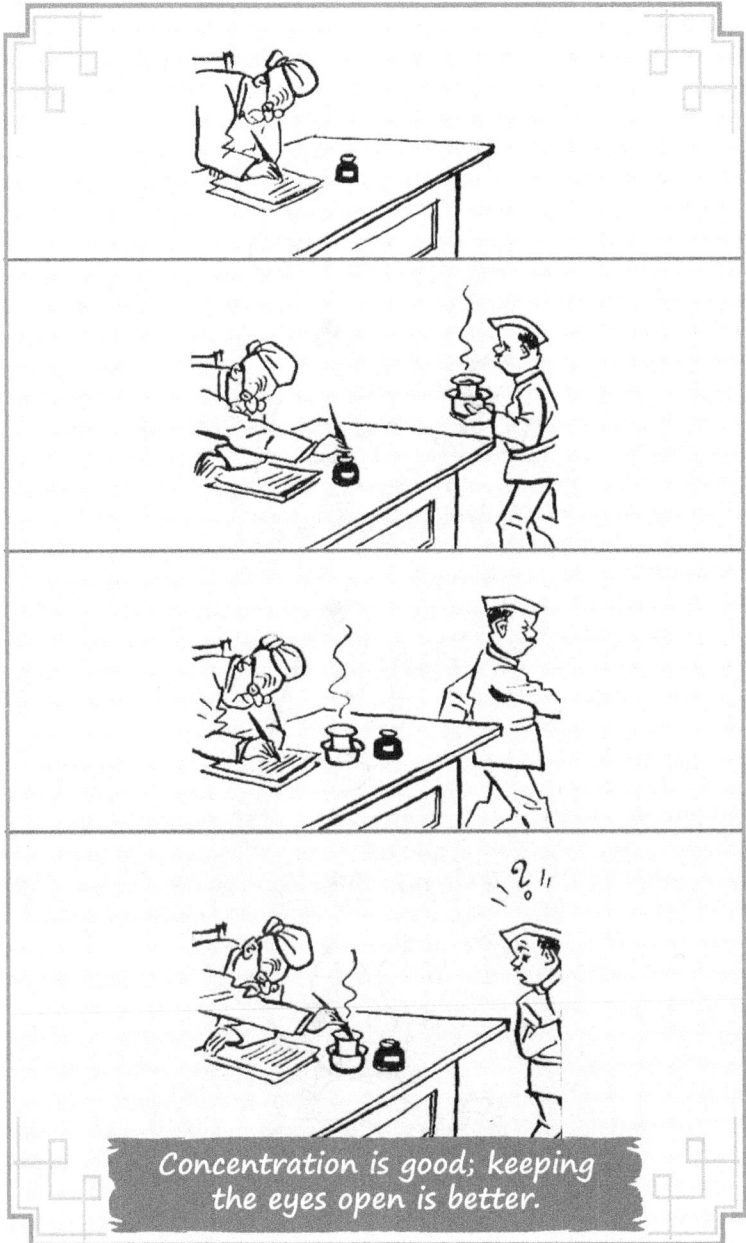

Concentration is good; keeping
the eyes open is better.

Reduce inventory,
the system works.

Good wares cannot be
sold in bad spots.

Music can foster
plants. For example...

The overgrown protégé
silences his mentor.

Window-shopping
allures but deludes.

Self-help is the best help.

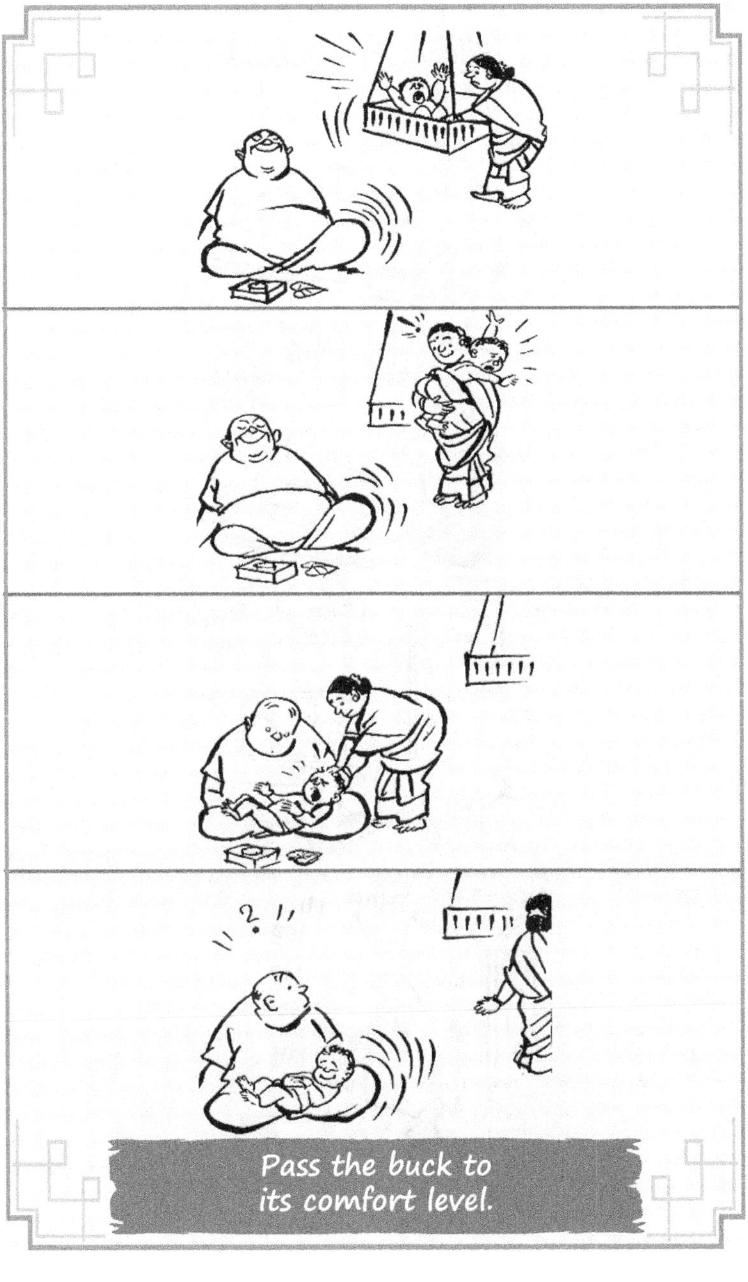

Pass the buck to
its comfort level.

Etiquette is to avoid instant responses.

In some gifts, the giver gains.

Brush aside the threats
with a threatening brush.

Kreech, kirr-ch.
Hoi, Hoi, Creech
Tup, Tup, up- Ghee, Tup

Akashvaani...
All India Radio's
programmes are
over for the day.
Our next...

**Some products turn useful
the moment you dump them.**

Your unintended wastes
clothe others.

Retaliate from a safe haven.

Your prey takes its own prey.

Beware of a third party grab.

Application matters,
not just study.

Turn your tool upside down,
it could serve better.

**Ears could mislead;
track the source.**

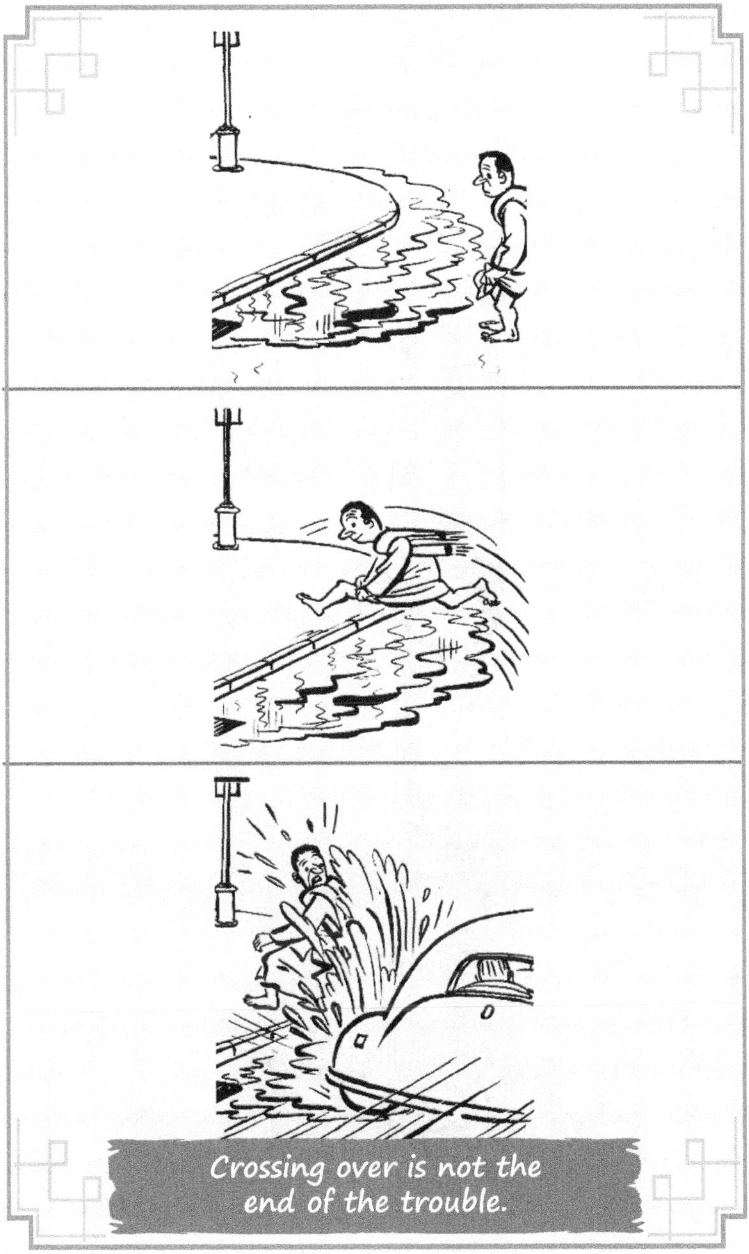

Crossing over is not the
end of the trouble.

Those bound to awaken
others shall not sleep.

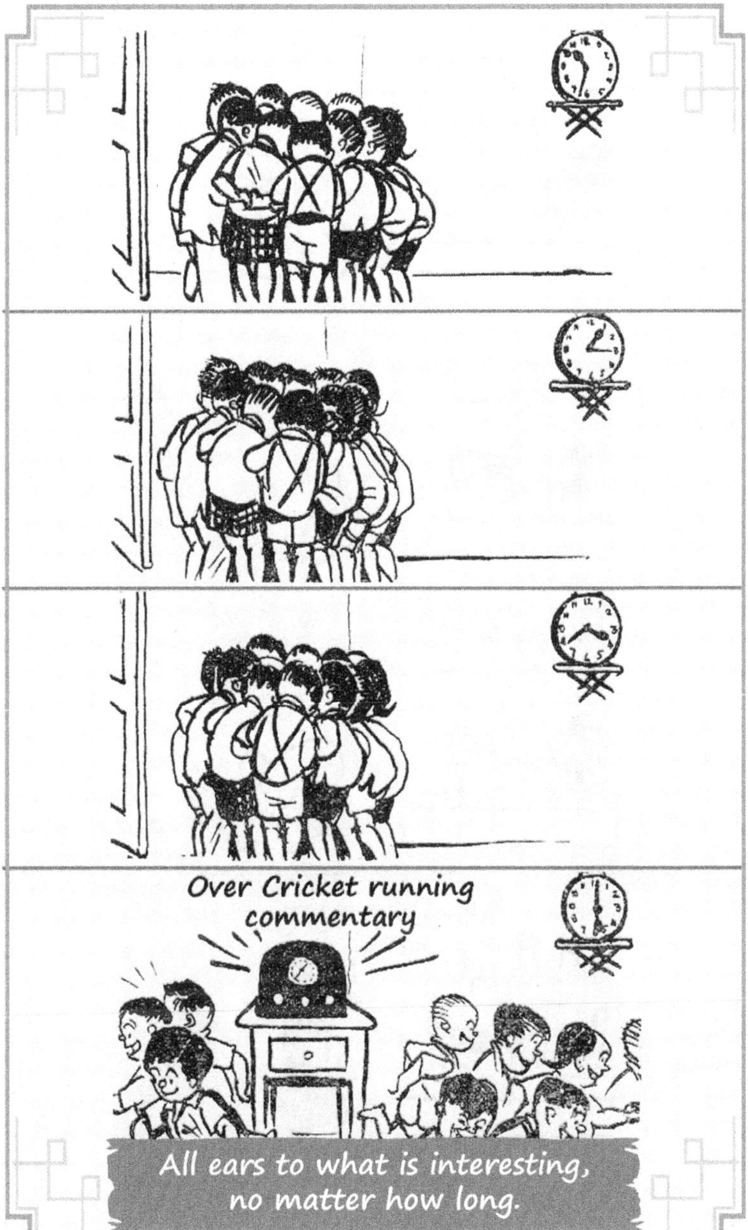

Over Cricket running commentary

All ears to what is interesting,
no matter how long.

The more you talk,
the less you are heard.

Mock up, for the make-up.

United, rats can bell the cat.

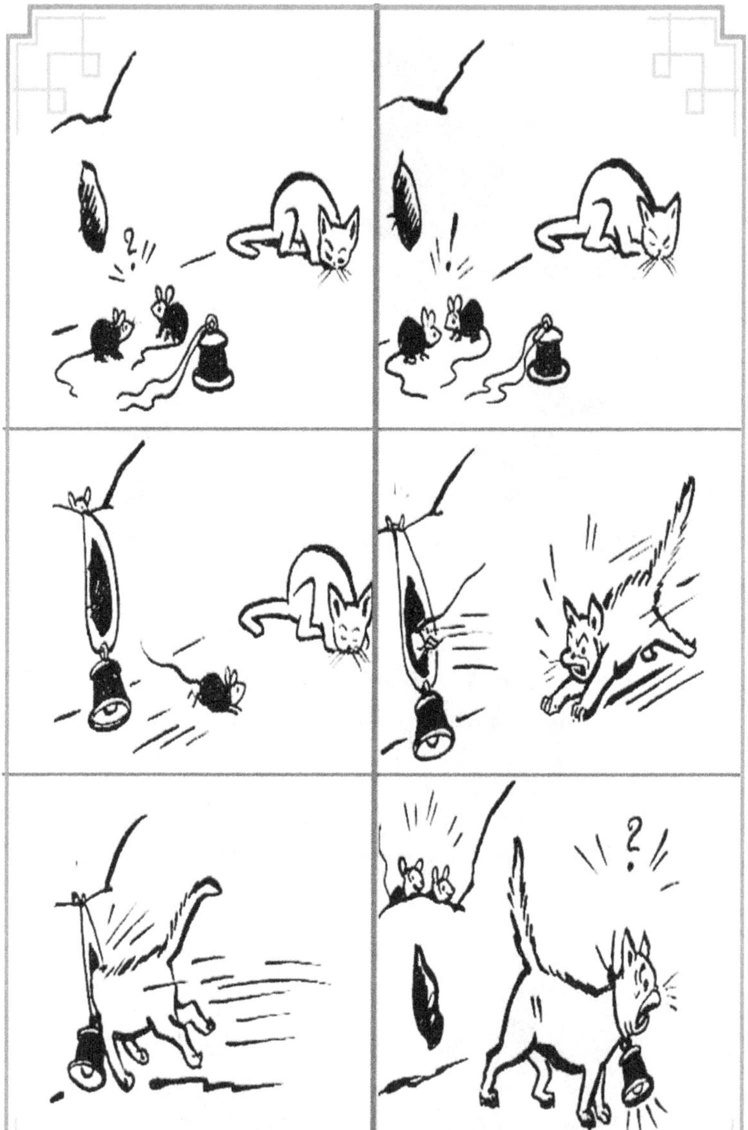

For the semblance of reality,
faking needs simulation.

Temple Fire Walk

A familiar fire scorches less.

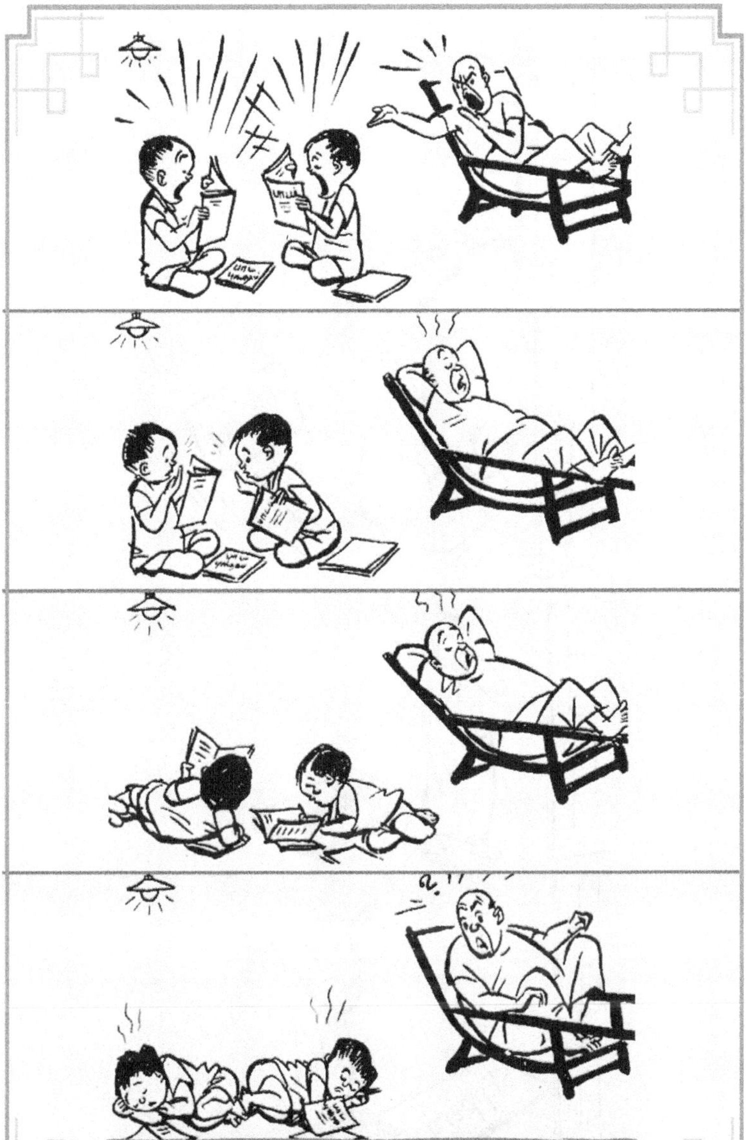

Buy peace before you sleep.

Warning signs pop up after the fall.

When at risk, deploy
your professional skill.

All talents that please
others do not feed you.

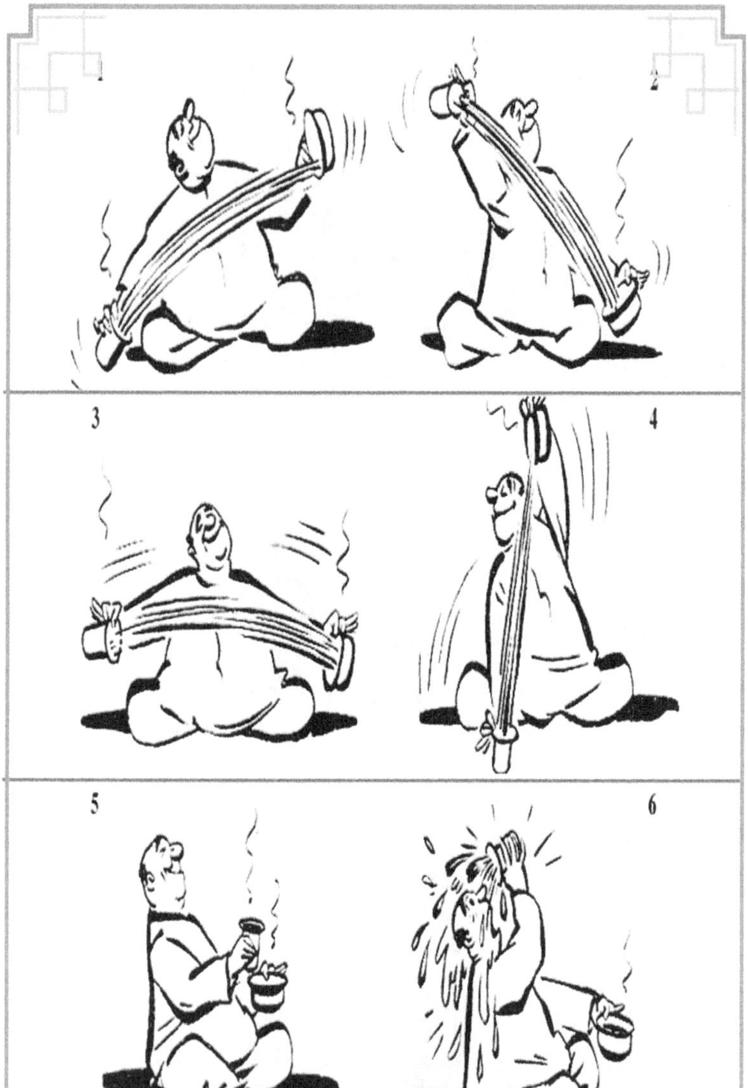

Comfort is not in what is
given, but what is taken.

Child is the father of man!

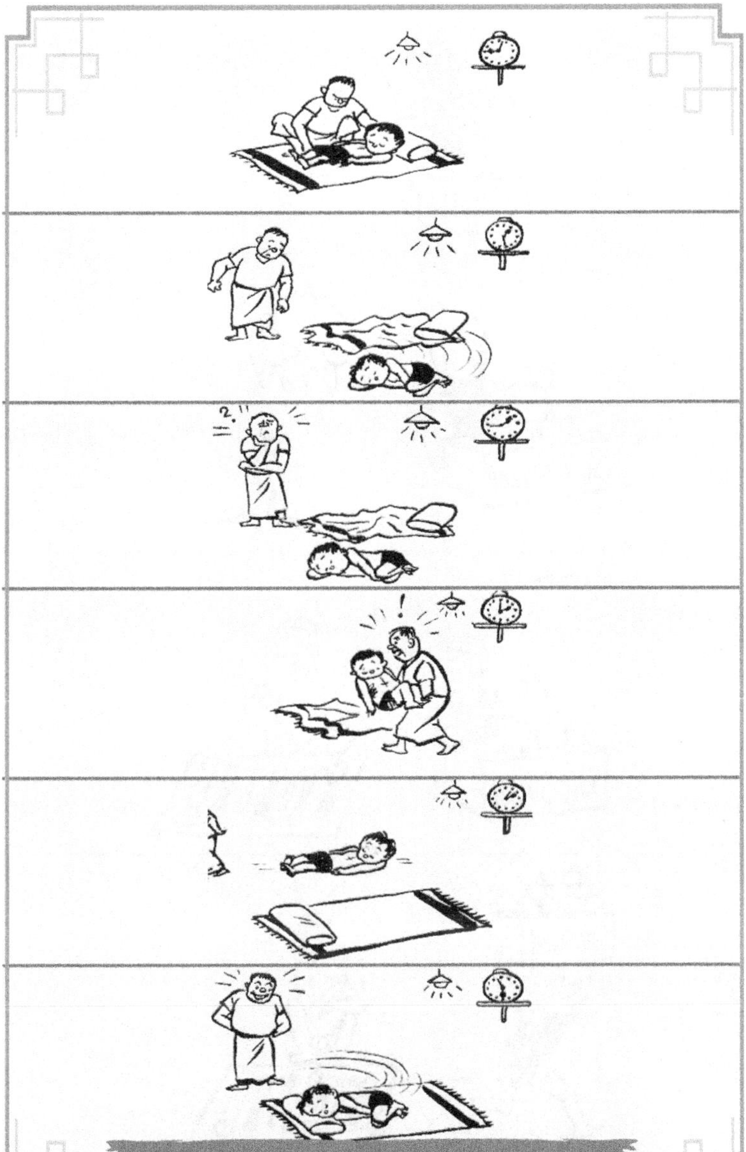

Your care kills other's sleep.

Shun bad neighbourhood in business.

The brainy passes through any obstacle.

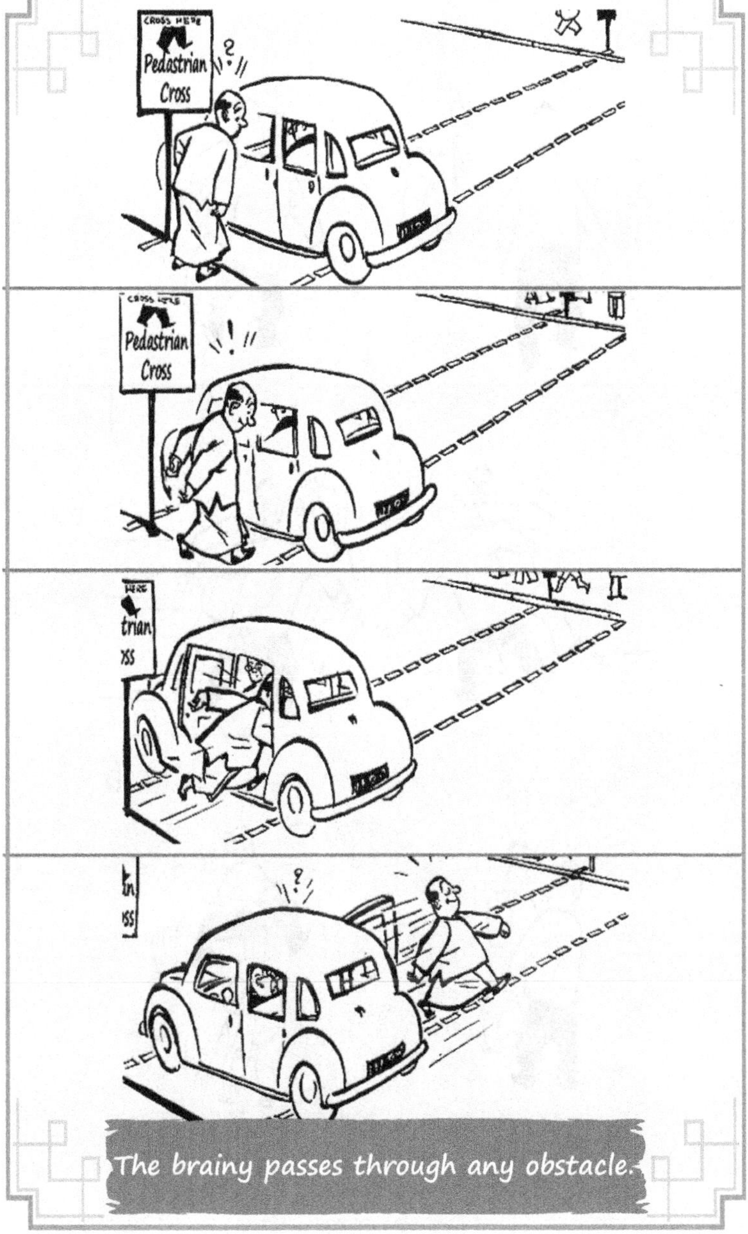

When you can't side-step,
jump over!

After demolition, contrive illusion.

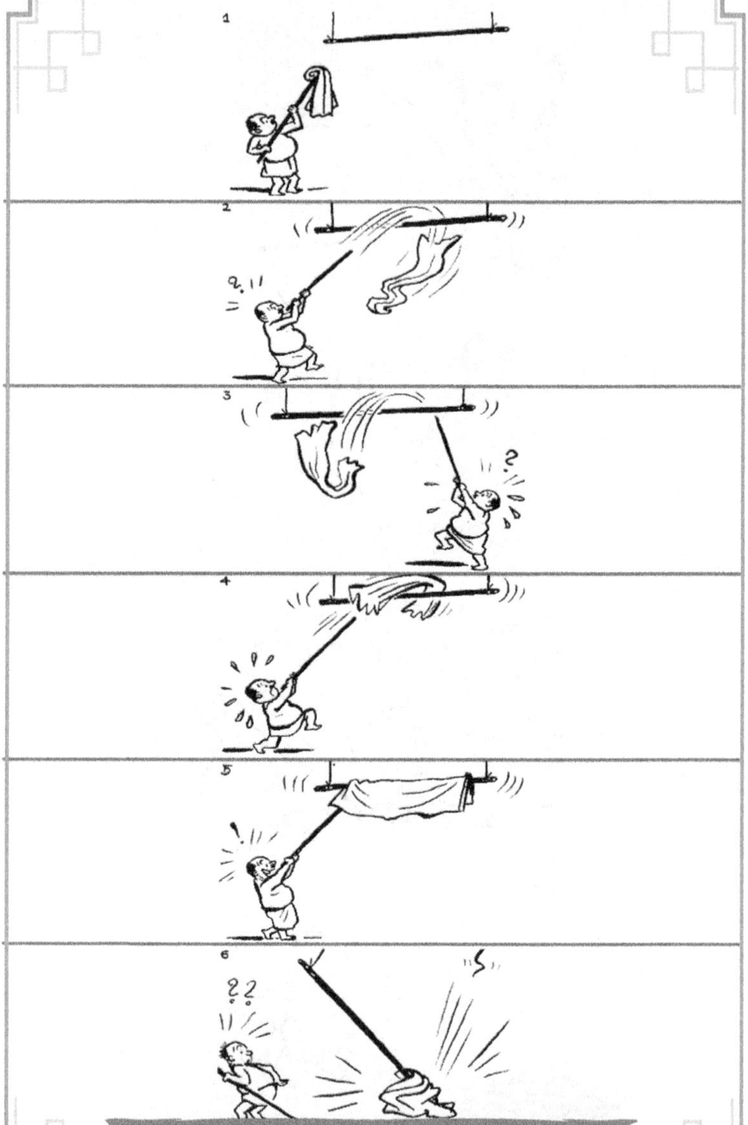

Improper know-how,
damages the infrastructure.

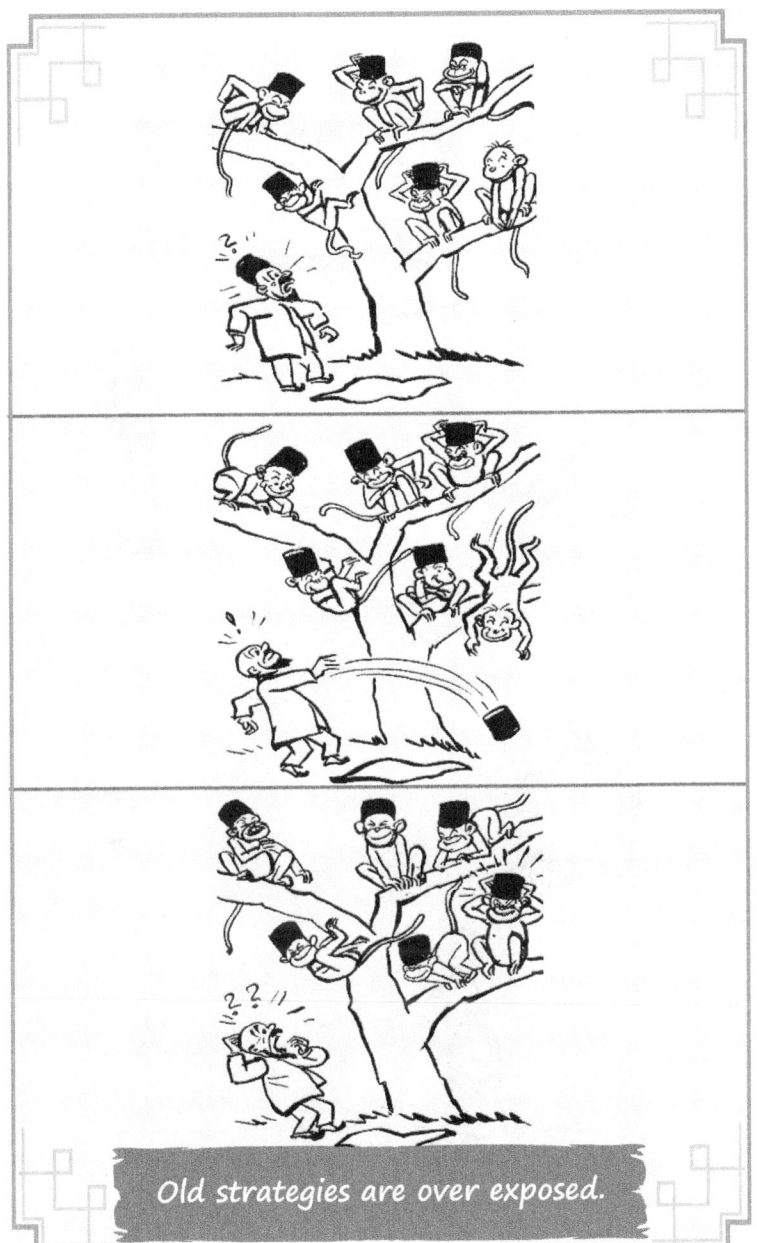

Old strategies are over exposed.

With help around,
you never miss the bus.

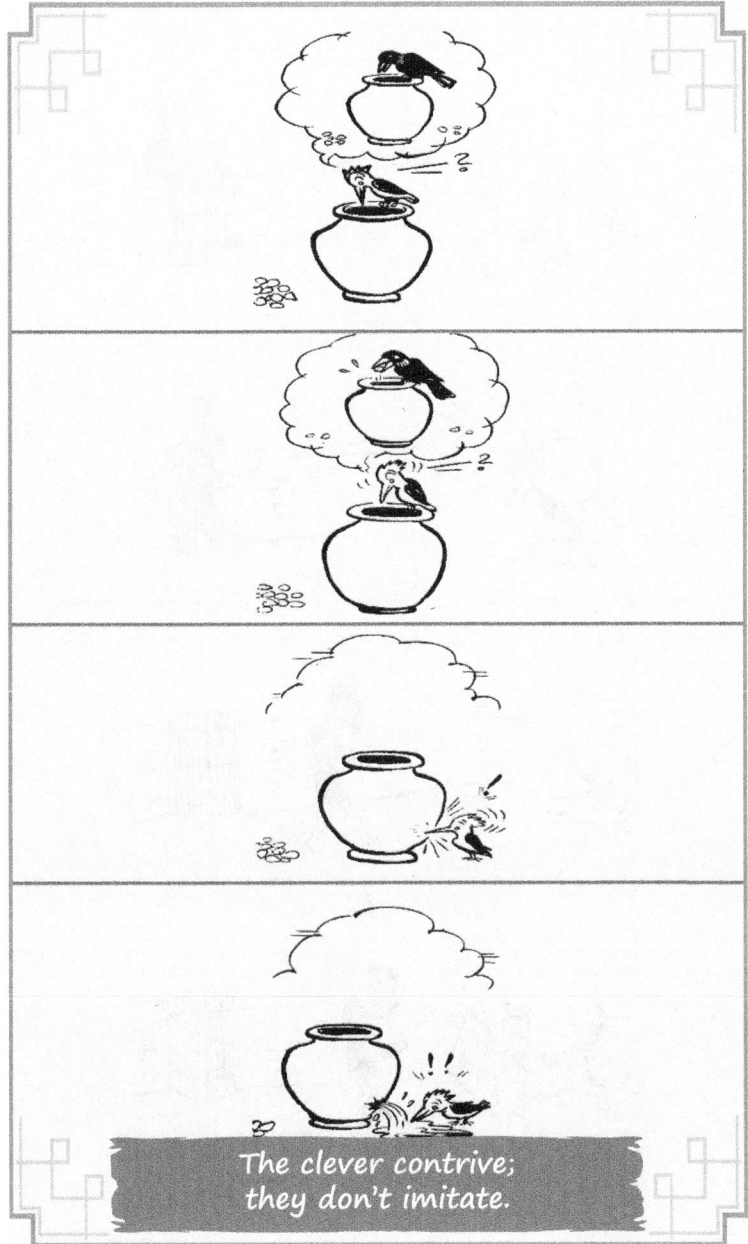

The clever contrive;
they don't imitate.

No matter who you are,
get introduced rightly!

Grab attention with
the inventory at hand.

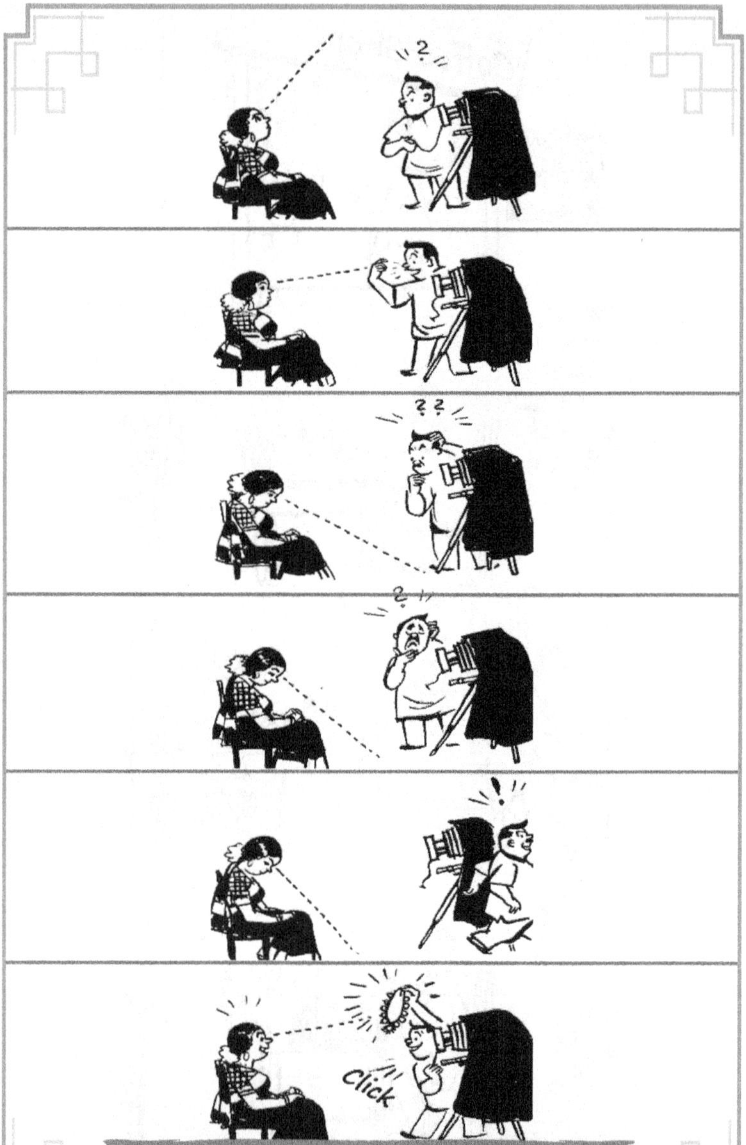

Incentives induce intended results.

Withdraw when you know you will lose.

Know how to deploy the
wherewithal in exigencies.

Curiosity over the affairs
next door is never abated.

The fun ends the moment
you realize your loss.

When people behave contrary to instructions, instruct the contrary.

Use the nearest hide-out.

Sales pick up when
truth is on discount.

More often you don't know
who you take care of.

Don't quarrel with your tools.
Just convert them.

Help others, to be out-helped.

Don't be ear-led;
cast your eyes around.

**Music is not food
of love for musicians!**

Necessity is the mother
of niche marketing.

Your systems are no systems for others.

Old age is second childhood!

**Contribute in kind,
it is also value addition.**

Dreams end up in aching wake up.

Art lives outside the gallery.

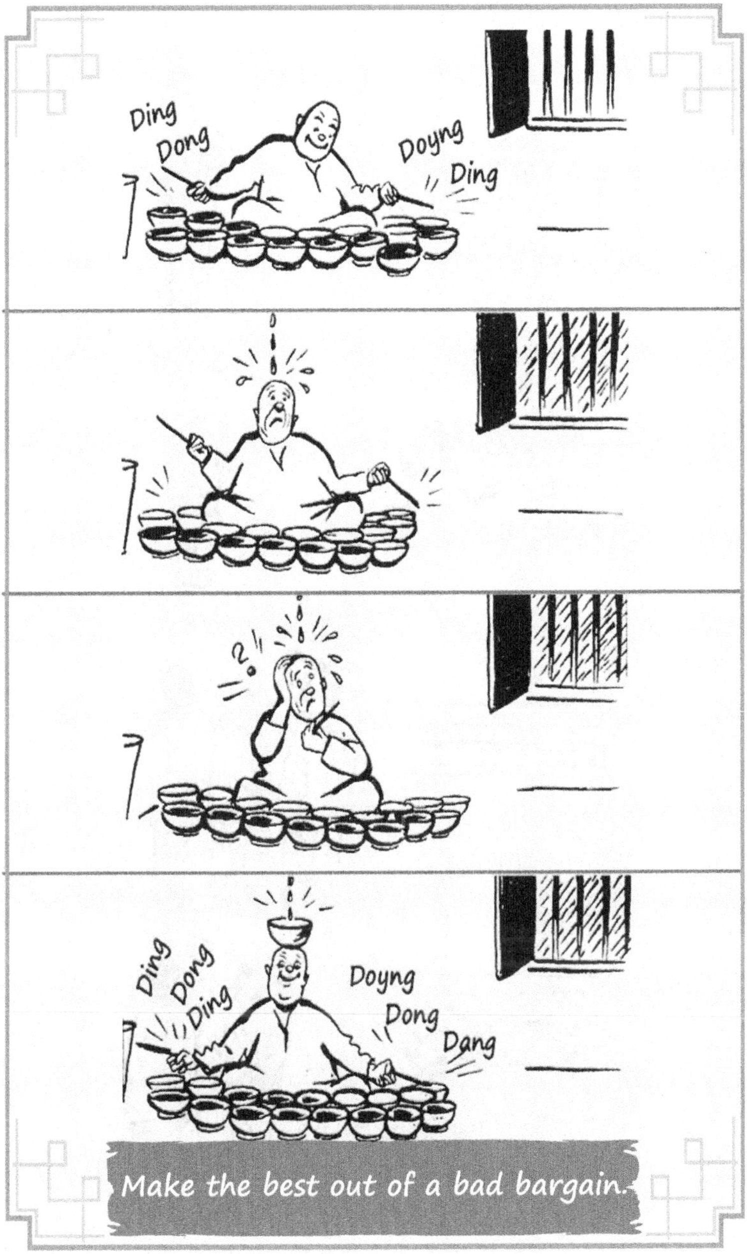

Make the best out of a bad bargain.

If there is no vacancy, contrive one.

Help is seldom reciprocated.
So be helped first!

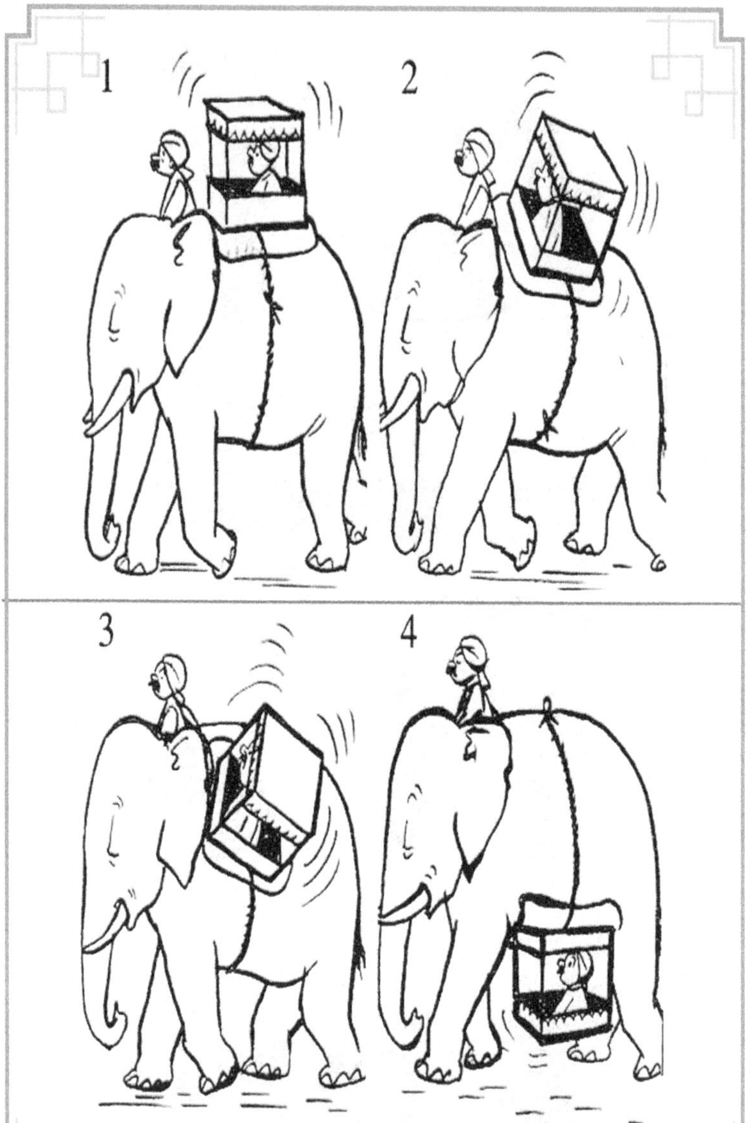

78

They slide and sling in comfort.

Made in the USA
Monee, IL
07 July 2026

56552352R00167